Getting Started

A Guide to Implementation

Fluency Foundations
Units A–J

Marilyn Sprick, Ann Watanabe, Karen Akiyama-Paik, and Shelley V. Jones

Sopris West®

13 12 11 10 09 08   2 3 4 5 6 7

ISBN 13: 978-1-60218-511-1
ISBN 10: 1-60218-511-5

166713

Printed in the United States of America
Published and Distributed by

Sopris West®
EDUCATIONAL SERVICES

A Cambium Learning Company

4093 Specialty Place • Longmont, CO 80504 • 303-651-2829
www.sopriswest.com

Dear Teachers:

With *Fluency Foundations*, we are excited to provide second grade students with a 40-day fluency program. With this solid foundation under them, even students who normally "get by" can excel. The program is specifically designed to build automaticity with known skills and increase reading fluency. Our goal is that every child not only learns to read, but learns to read well.

With *Fluency Foundations*, we are also pleased to provide third grade students with a program that will help them master essential first grade skills—skills needed to move forward toward grade level reading.

We have written *Fluency Foundations* with a continued passion for doing what's best for kids. Our first priority has been to maintain a research-based core while simultaneously working to captivate the kids with engaging content.

Our Guiding Principles

- Children need to read well to feel like they belong in the world of school—and in their communities. Reading well gives young people the confidence and ability to seek opportunities not afforded those who read poorly.
- Despite differences in backgrounds and abilities, every child deserves to receive instruction that meets his or her individual needs.
- Teaching young children to read well requires: (a) carefully designed programs, (b) dedicated and skillful teachers, (c) sufficient instructional time, and (d) professional collaboration.
- Teachers deserve finely tuned instructional tools to meet the varied needs of the children they serve.

Our best to you all,

Marilyn Sprick

Ann Watanabe

Karen Akiyama-Paik

Shelley V. Jones

"Learning is not attained by chance. It must be sought for with ardor and attended to with diligence."

—Abigail Adams
(1744–1818)

Dedicated to:

- The children who keep us humble and always learning more

- The teachers who go the extra mile for the kids they serve

- The researchers who inform our practice

Acknowledgements:

- The staff members at Pacific Northwest Publishing who assisted with the painstaking programming and preparation of manuscripts

- The editors at Sopris West who polished and fine tuned at the finish

- The designers and artists who shared their talents—making this program an invitation to read

- The writers who added their voices to our storybooks

- Paula Rich, who wrote many of the bazillion fluency and assessment passages, each with a unique little twist to keep kids interested

- The teachers who field tested, weathered draft copies, and shared the accomplishments of their kids

- Nancy Wing, second grade field test teacher, who put off retirement to be a gracious guardian of our goals to produce a teacher- and student-friendly curriculum

- Jonelle Agliam Flight, who generously provided feedback as a master second grade teacher

- Anita Archer, who has been friend, mentor, and a teacher to us all

- Randy Sprick, author of the Safe and Civil Schools series, who has allowed us to share his expertise in teaching behavioral expectations and whose expertise in motivating children is always present in our scripting

- Our families, who cheered us on and patiently gave us the time we needed to do our best for kids

Marilyn Sprick, M.S., is the senior author of the *Read Well* series. With degrees in psychology, education, and special education, Marilyn has worked as a general education teacher, Title 1 learning specialist, and special education teacher. As a consultant, Marilyn has worked with thousands of teachers across the country—adapting curriculum and instruction to better meet the needs of all students. The *Read Well* and *Read Well Spelling and Writing Conventions* projects have allowed Marilyn to bring together her expertise as a research-based reading teacher, curriculum specialist, staff developer, and writer. From Eugene, Oregon, Marilyn and Randy Sprick co-direct Teaching Strategies, Inc.— a nationally recognized group of consultants who work with schools to improve student responsibility and academic success.

Ann Watanabe, M.S., has worked in education for more than 30 years as a special education teacher, general education teacher, resource teacher, and reading coach. Her experience includes working with schools on school improvement and observing and consulting with teachers to improve behavior management and instructional delivery. Ann provides consultation and training in beginning reading, effective instruction, and a range of supplemental and intervention reading programs. She has developed trainings in reading and effective instruction and is a coauthor of the Hawaii State Literacy Tutor Training Program. Ann has presented at district, state, and national levels and is the recipient of a national Excellence in Education Staff Development award. She is also a National Board Certified Teacher in Literacy: Reading-Language Arts/Early and Middle Childhood.

Karen Akiyama-Paik, M.Ed., has worked in schools as a general education teacher, a special education teacher, reading coach, and consultant. As a state and district resource teacher, Karen has provided ongoing consultation and support to school staffs in school improvement and staff development. She has trained and supervised numerous teachers in research-based literacy instructional practices statewide. Karen is a coauthor of the Hawaii State Literacy Tutor Training Program used to train many paraprofessionals in effective practices for teaching reading. Karen has supervised grants and helped develop statewide curriculum frameworks for language arts and reading. She has field-tested *Read Well Fluency Foundations* and *Read Well Plus* with a high-risk population of remedial students.

Shelley V. Jones, M.Mus., has worked in schools as a Title 1 teacher, reading specialist, kindergarten teacher, and music specialist. In her role as a reading specialist, Shelley has supervised, trained, and provided ongoing consultation to staff members as they successfully implemented *Read Well* with a high-risk population. As a coauthor, Shelley has brought her knowledge of the importance of practice in developing expertise and her knowledge of the needs of young children and teachers to the authoring of *Read Well K* and *2* and the revision of *Read Well 1*. Using her professional music background, Shelley has also shared her talents in the creation of the *Read Well 2* CD of Songs.

Table of Contents

Who Is Fluency Foundations For?

Fluency Foundations **is a component of** ***Read Well 2.*** **This fast-paced program provides mastery-based instruction of first grade reading skills.**

Second Grade • Core

Students who place in *Fluency Foundations* in second grade have learned basic first grade skills but would benefit from a quick review to build fluency.

What's next?

When students complete *Fluency Foundations,* first grade skills will have been established as a foundation for future learning. *Fluency Foundations* students continue into *Read Well 2,* finishing the school year at or above grade level.

Third Grade • Core Replacement or Supplemental

Students who place in *Fluency Foundations* in third grade have learned basic first grade skills but would benefit from a quick review to build fluency. These students are reading significantly below grade level. With *Fluency Foundations,* they will master first grade skills.

What's next?

These students proceed into *Read Well 1 Plus.* By the end of the school year, they will be reading trade books like the Magic Treehouse Series. Some of these students will be ready to work at grade level; others will require continued intensive and systematic instruction.

Section

1

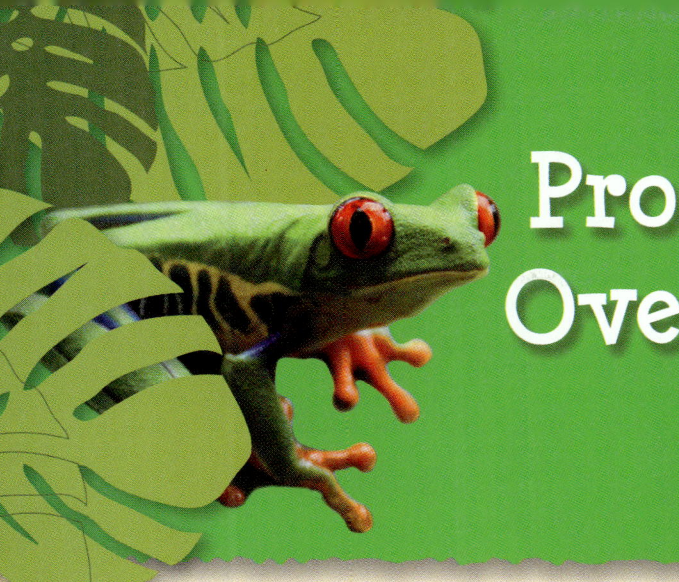

Program Overview

In this section:

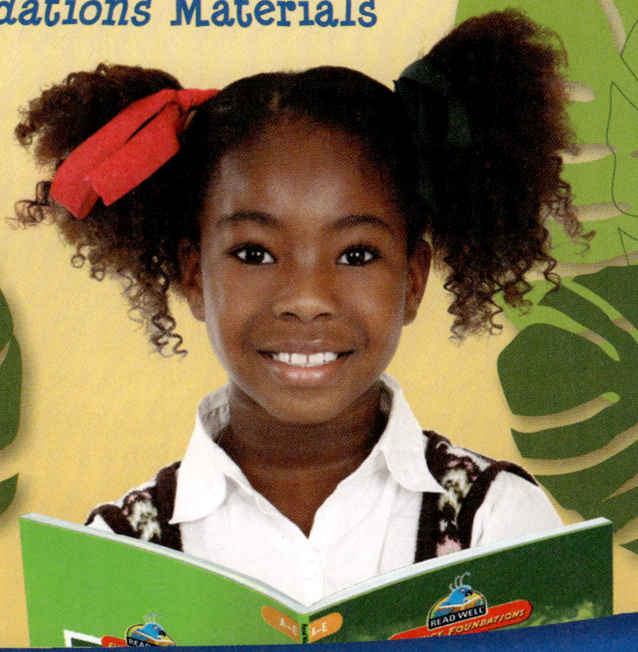

What *Fluency Foundations* Kids Can Do

Fluency Foundations is a joy to teach and is fun for kids.

As with other *Read Well* programs, *Fluency Foundations* was built on findings from scientifically based reading research. Because research studies are typically short term and limited to a specific area of reading, we also field-tested to ensure that the program improved student achievement, was a joy to teach, and was fun for kids.

> ### STRONG IN CONTENT
>
> *"In 30-plus years of teaching, I had never taught a program that so successfully gave students the skills they needed to continue to learn to read.* Fluency Foundations *is the "fix-it" program for the student who needs that extra push to become a strong and independent reader. While being engaged by interesting and motivating stories, students were firming up their fluency. At the same time, they acquired a strong foundation in phonemic awareness, phonics, vocabulary, and comprehension strategies. This foundation allowed them to continue into* Read Well 2 *with ease. By the end of the school year, my students were reading well above a third grade level!"*
>
> —Second grade field-test teacher

Student Achievement

Field Testing. Field testing of *Fluency Foundations* in conjunction with *Read Well 2* was conducted at three high-risk schools and included eight second grade classrooms. Data derived were strictly for the purpose of evaluation, not research. All schools participated in a walk-to-read model with 60 minutes of instruction provided per day. Across all sites, students exceeded expected gains when compared with a nationally normed sample. Field test data demonstrate the promise that these programs provide.

Fluency Foundations was field tested with a total of 33 second grade students in three schools. Groups ranged in size from 7 to 14 students. These students gained an average of 35 words correct per minute across 9–10 weeks of instruction.

According to Hasbrouck and Tindal (2006), the average weekly improvement for second grade students is 1.1 to 1.2 words correct per minute. *Fluency Foundations* students exceeded expectations by improving an average of 3.5 words correct per minute per week.

What *RW2 Fluency Foundations* Kids Can Read

Across Field Test Sites: In the fall of their second grade year, field test students were administered the Woodcock Reading Mastery Short Scale. These students averaged a grade equivalency of 2.35 in Total Reading (a combined measure of Word Identification and Passage Comprehension). By spring, these students averaged a 3.75 grade equivalency, a gain of 1.4—nearly a year and a half of grade equivalence in one school year.

In Passage Comprehension, field test students began with an average grade equivalency of 1.76. By the spring, these students averaged 3.39. They had gained 1.63—over a year and a half of grade equivalence in one school year.

***Fluency Foundations* Students:** Students who began in *Fluency Foundations* in the fall of their second grade year averaged a 2.27 grade equivalence in total reading. By the spring, these students averaged a 3.82. They gained 1.55 in one school year.

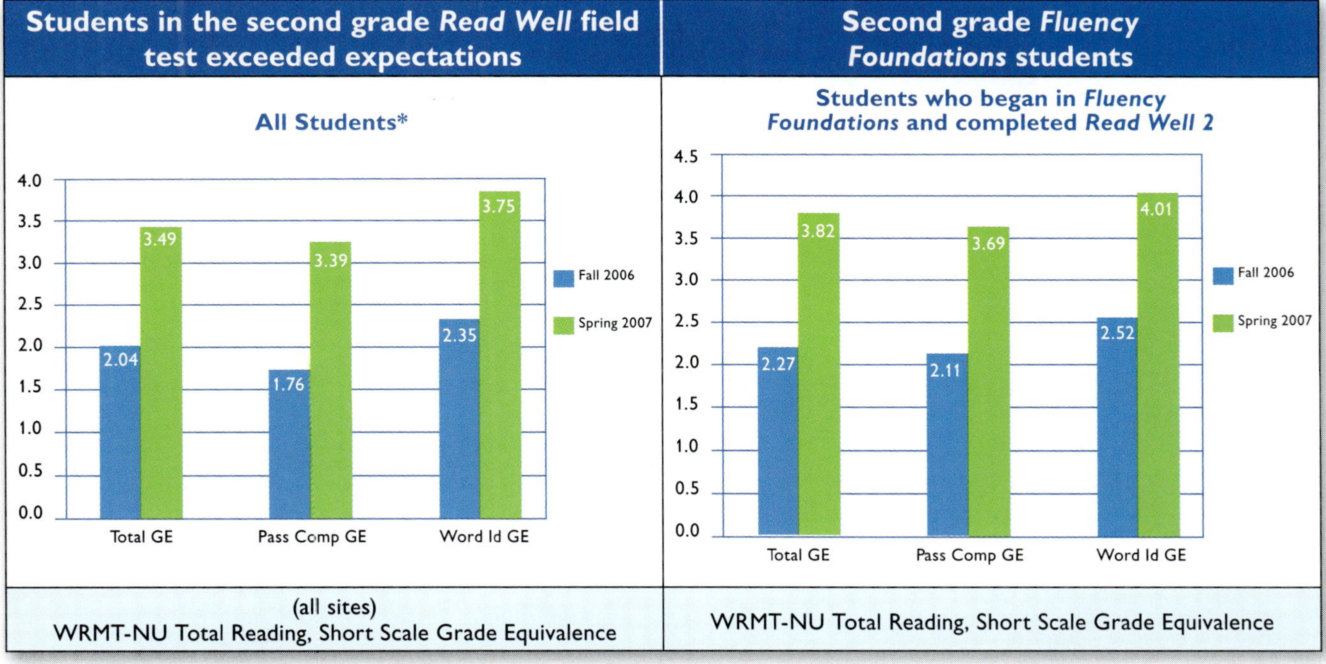

Woodcock Reading Mastery Test Normative Update (WRMT-NU) Short Scale was selected because it is nationally normed, individually administered, and includes subtests on passage comprehension as well as word identification.

Students in field testing . . .

Site 1: Small city	Site 2: Large inner city	Site 3: Small rural town
• 76% free and reduced lunch • 40% minority • 18.1% English Language Learners (ELL)	• 81.5% free and reduced lunch • 75% minority • 23.1% ELL	• 41% free and reduced lunch • 13% minority • 7.6% ELL

* **Students were placed appropriately into *Read Well 2*, *Fluency Foundations*, or *Read Well 1*.**

A Foundation for Reading Well

Second Grade • *Fluency Foundations* into *Read Well 2*

When second grade students place in *Fluency Foundations*, they will end the year at or above grade level. Students begin the year building decoding skills in simple stories, but they finish the year reading sophisticated text about the Great Barrier Reef and the human body, as well as the popular trade book *Flat Stanley*. These students will read words such as: approximately, phytoplankton, and cerebellum. By the end of the school year, students who begin second grade in *Fluency Foundations* are ready for third grade!

Fluency Foundations, Unit B, The Cricket and the Ant

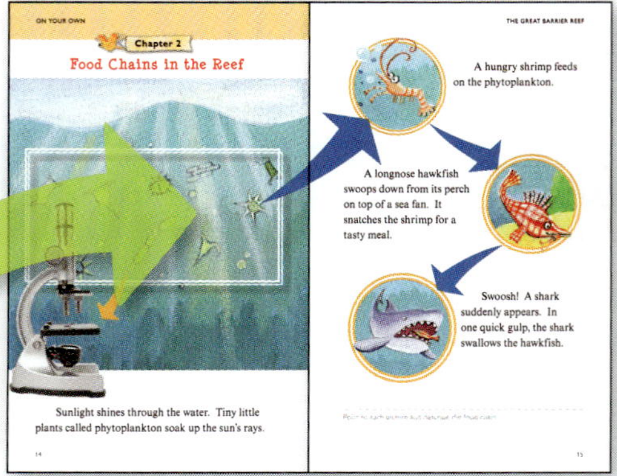

Read Well 2, Unit 18, Chains in the Reef

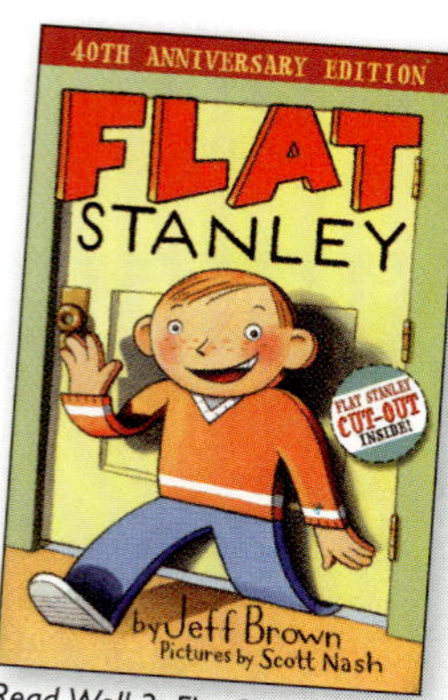

Read Well 2, Flat Stanley

Third Grade • *Fluency Foundations* into *Read Well 1 Plus*

When third grade students place in *Fluency Foundations*, they will be approaching grade level by the end of the school year. These students may require more than 40 days to master the skills in *Fluency Foundations*. If these students proceed into *Fluency Foundations* and complete *Read Well 1 Plus* at mastery, they will score anywhere from a 2.7 grade equivalency to a 4.7 grade equivalency on the Woodcock Reading Mastery NU, Short Scale, Total Reading. If *Read Well 1 Plus* is not available, our recommendation would be to test for placement into *Read Well 2*.

Fluency Foundations, Units A–E, Unit F

Read Well 1 Plus, Unit 49

Scientifically Based Reading Research

Why *Fluency Foundations* Works

Reading is based on a foundation of oral language. Although oral language is developed naturally, reading is a learned skill, a complex mental activity that requires a sophisticated interaction between language, thought, and print.

The graphic organizer below reflects the objectives and strategies incorporated in *Read Well*. From and through oral language, *Read Well Kindergarten* and *Read Well 1* provide explicit and systematic instruction in the five areas of instructional focus identified by researchers as being critical to reading with understanding. On a daily basis, students receive instruction in phonemic awareness, phonics, comprehension strategies, vocabulary, and fluency.*

In *Fluency Foundations*, instruction and practice focuses on building mastery of *Read Well 1's* basic phonics sequence while increasing reading fluency. Though the emphasis is on decoding and fluency, students work in balanced lessons that include vocabulary and comprehension building. The next pages provide snapshots of how *Fluency Foundations* addresses each area of instructional focus: Phonological Awareness and Phonics, Phonics, Vocabulary, Comprehension, and Fluency.

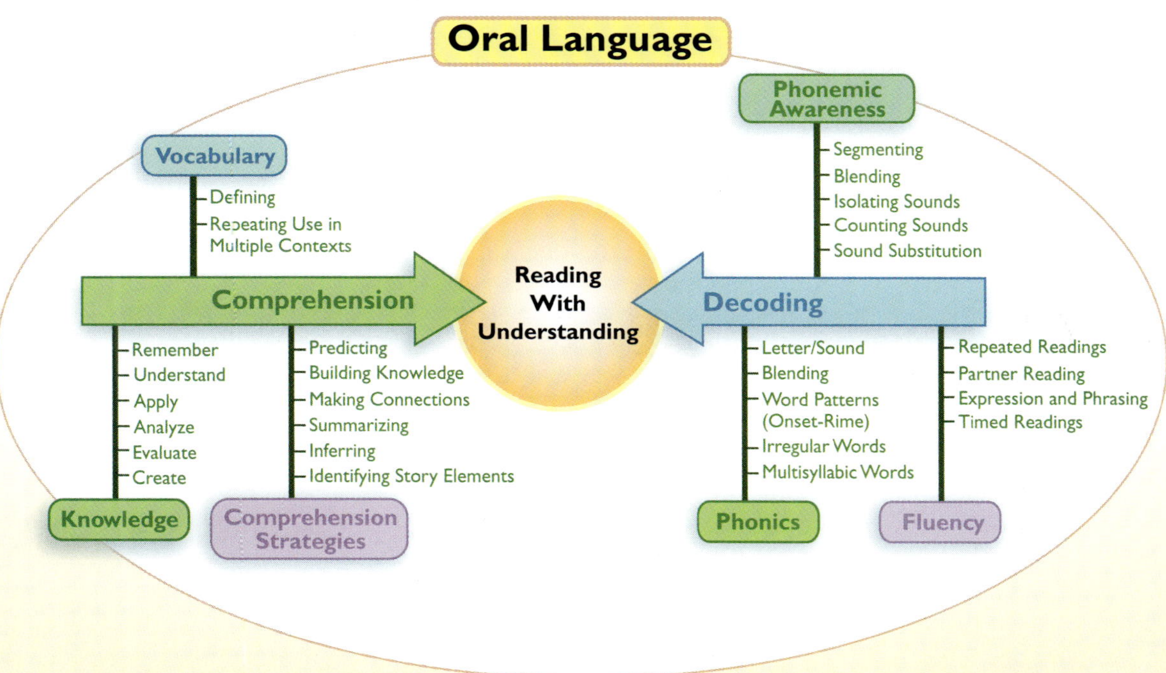

Graphic organizer adapted from Archer, 2000.

*** Adams, 1990; Anderson, Hiebert, Scott, & Wilkinson, 1985; Armbruster, Lehn, & Osborn, 2001; National Reading Panel, 2000; Rayner, Foorman, Perfetti, Pesetsky, & Seidenberg, 2001; Torgesen, 2004. See the reference list on page 166.**

Phonological Awareness and Phonics

Research Snapshot

Systematic Phonics and Comprehension

After an extensive review of scientifically based reading research, the National Reading Panel (2000) concluded that "growth in word-reading skills is strongly enhanced by systematic phonics instruction . . . . Growth in reading comprehension is also boosted by systematic phonics instruction for younger students and reading-disabled students. These findings should dispel any belief that teaching phonics systematically to young children interferes with their ability to read and comprehend text" (Sec. 2, p. 86).

Phonics instruction improves comprehension.

Phonological Awareness

Most students who enter *Fluency Foundations* have mastered phonemic awareness skills—the ability to hear and manipulate sounds in words.* In *Fluency Foundations*, phonemic awareness training continues within the context of phonics activities. (Extra Practice lessons provide additional phonemic awareness training for students who need extra assistance.)

Phonological training continues in *Fluency Foundations* with rhyming words (e.g., bought, thought, brought). Students also learn to chunk and count syllables.

Phonics

Students who place in *Fluency Foundations* quickly review *Read Well 1's* basic letter/sound associations and combinations blending of pattern words, words with endings, and simple multisyllabic words.

High-Frequency Words

High-frequency words are taught within the decoding sequence.

Fry's Instant Words	First 100	First 200	First 300	First 400	First 500
Fluency Foundations	99	183	261	318	371

* Second grade students should continue to use segmentation skills for the purpose of spelling. *Read Well 2 Spelling and Writing Conventions* provides daily training in these skills.

Research Snapshot

The Long-Term Importance of Word Reading Skills

"If children do not acquire good word reading skills early in elementary school, they will be cut off from the rich knowledge sources available in print, and this may be particularly unfortunate for children who are already weak in verbal knowledge and ability" (Torgesen, 2000, p. 58).

Phonics instruction is explicit, and stories are fully decodable.

Fluency Foundations systematically builds automaticity with letter/sound associations. For students who place in *Fluency Foundations*, each 4-day unit focuses on a set of sounds introduced in *Read Well 1*.

Fluency Foundations, Skill Sequence and Topics

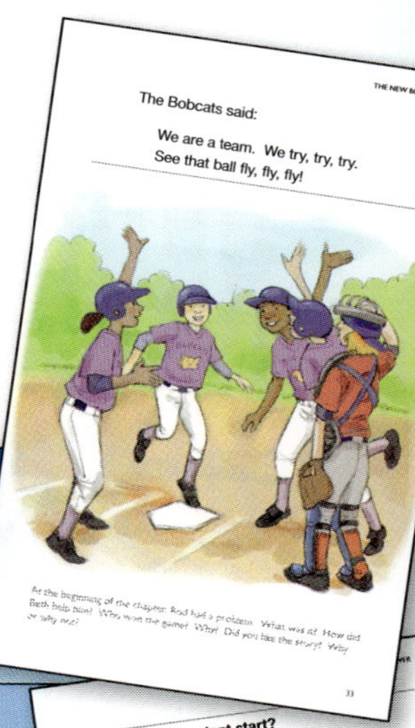

Unit	Review of *Read Well 1*	Sound Sequence Focus	Story Titles and Genres
A	Units 16, 17, 18	oo, ar, wh	**The Song Contest** • Fiction, Imaginative
B	Units 19, 20, 21	Ee (short), -y (fly), Ll	**Aesop's Fables** • Fiction, Classic Tales
C	Units 22, 23, 24, 25	Oo, Bb, all, Gg, Ff	**The New Bobcat** • Fiction, Realistic Narrative
D	Units 26, 27	Uu, er, oo	**Harriet Tubman Escapes** • Nonfiction, Historical Narrative **Freedom Fighter** • Nonfiction, Historical Narrative
E	Units 28, 29	a (schwa), Yy, Pp, ay	**Little Brother Tuck** • Fiction, Realistic Narrative
F	Units 30, 31, 32, 33	Vv, qu, Jj, or, Xx	**Volcanoes on Earth** • Nonfiction, Expository; Nonfiction, Historical Narrative
G	Units 34, 35	a_e, Zz, -y (baby)	**The Case of the Missing Cards** • Fiction, Imaginative
H	Units 35, 36	i_e, ou, ow (cow)	**Wacky Weather Facts** • Fiction, Imaginative; Nonfiction, Expository
I	Units 37, 38	ch, ai, o_e	**Chaz and the Magic Beans** • Fiction, Imaginative **From Seed to Flower** • Nonfiction, Expository
J	Unit 38	igh, ir	**Irma the Discontented Cow** • Nonfiction, Expository; Fiction, Imaginative

Phonics

Daily decoding practice provides explicit instruction and practice.

Daily decoding practice introduces new words from the unit's stories, strengthens known skills, and builds new skills at an appropriate pace. *Fluency Foundations* Decoding Practice and Extra Practice lessons provide *systematic and explicit* daily practice. Valuable preparation time is not spent creating word lists!

DECODING EXERCISE COMPONENTS

Focus Sound
The sound ladder on the Unit Introduction page is used to introduce the focus sound(s) for the unit and to review sounds.

Sound Review
Sounds are reviewed daily for maintenance and fluency with the use of *Fluency Foundations* Sound Cards.

Shifty Word Blending
Students practice sound blending and learn that one letter makes a difference in word recognition.

Accuracy and Fluency
Skills are practiced first for accuracy and then for fluency.

Focus Sound Practice
Focus sounds are practiced within words as students identify the sound and then the word.

Mixed Practice
Review sounds are practiced within words as students identify the sound and then the word.

Bossy E
The silent e rule is reviewed systematically.

Rhyming Words
Students build fluency with word patterns.

Tricky Words
These irregular words do not conform to common letter/sound associations. All Tricky Words are introduced and practiced before Story Reading.

Phrases and Sentences
Students read phrases and sentences for accuracy and fluency.

Word Endings and Multisyllabic Words
Students learn to count syllables and practice big words in recognizable chunks and for fluency.

Sound and Tricky Word Dictation
Beginning in Unit A, student knowledge of individual sounds and Tricky Words is demonstrated through teacher-led dictation practice.

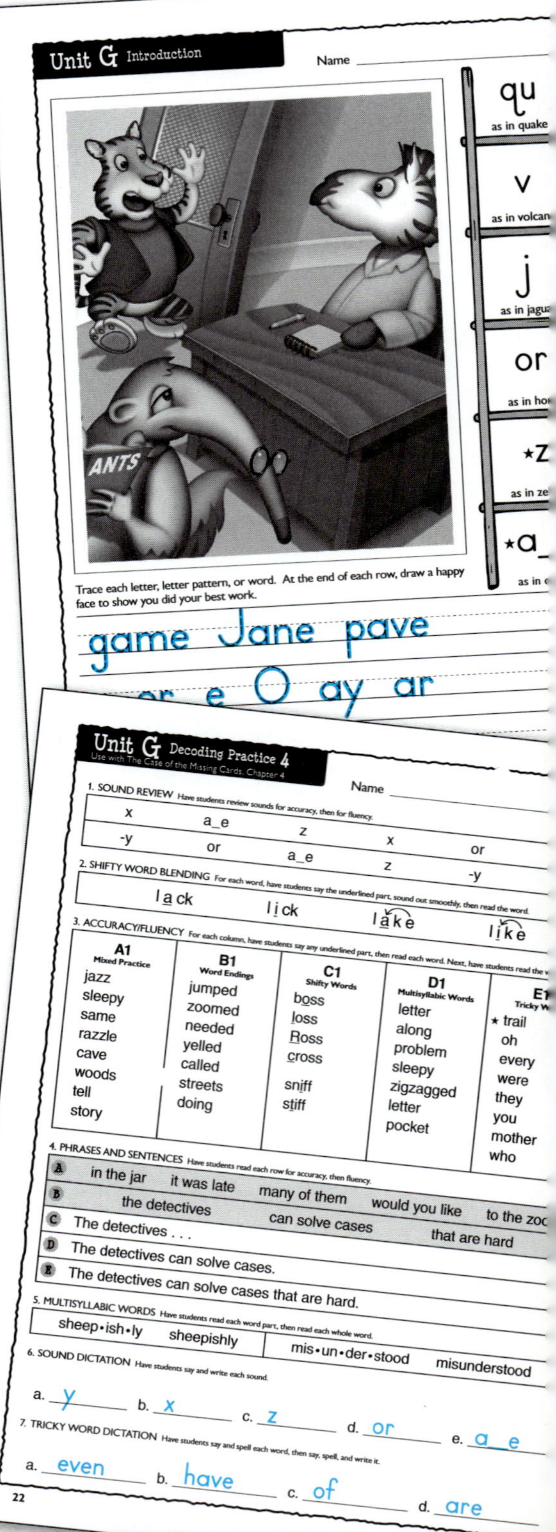

Research Snapshot

Vocabulary Instruction Improves Comprehension

There is consensus within the scientific community that vocabulary instruction leads to gains in comprehension (Baumann & Kame'enui, 1991; Beck, McKeown, & Kucan, 2002; National Reading Panel, 2000; Stahl, 2003).

Fluency Foundations teaches snazzy words, useful words, content-rich words . . .

The National Reading Panel (2000) recommended that vocabulary be provided through direct instruction, repetition and multiple exposures, learning in rich components, and active engagement in learning tasks.

Fluency Foundations introduces selected vocabulary words with direct instruction and then weaves use of the words through active engagement in multiple contexts.

Sample Unit Vocabulary Development

New Vocabulary from Unit A	New Vocabulary from Unit J
Nouns herbivore, carnivore, main character	**Nouns** omnivore
Descriptive Words (adjectives and adverbs) extraordinary	**Descriptive Words (adjectives and adverbs)** discontented

Vocabulary

Explicit Teaching of a Word Within a Unit and Multiple Exposures Across Units

VOCABULARY DEVELOPMENT OF . . . carnivore, herbivore, omnivore

Content words are included in *Fluency Foundations* many nonfiction selections. Students learn great words such as: volcano, erupt, magma, history, slave, fact, mantle, lava, omnivore, carnivore, and herbivore. Words like these are taught directly, used extensively within a unit, and then used across units—preparing the way for later work in science, social studies, and *Read Well 1 Plus* or *Read Well 2*.

Research Snapshot

Explicit Teaching of Vocabulary

- Teaching specific words before reading helps both vocabulary learning and reading comprehension.
- Extended instruction that promotes active engagement with vocabulary improves word learning.
- Repeated exposure to vocabulary in many contexts aids word learning.

(Armbruster, Lehr, & Osborne, 2003, p. 36)

Explicit Teaching Within a Unit

VOCABULARY DEVELOPMENT OF . . . mood

In *Fluency Foundations*, selected words are introduced, used in oral language, then reviewed in Comprehension and Skill Work, as appropriate.

Student-Friendly Definitions

The word "mood" is first introduced in the gray teacher text that appears in the storybook. Instruction precedes use of the word in the story. Questions prompt immediate use and application of the word by students.

Story Reading

Students read the words in context. Student interaction with the word "mood" is prompted by a teacher gray-text question later in the story.

Is Rod still in a sad *mood?* (No, Rod is not sad.)
How can you tell? (He has a big grin.)
How does he feel about the new team? (He likes them. He thinks they are cool.)
Why? (They are nice. They are good baseball players . . .)

Examples and Non-Examples

In their Comprehension and Skill Work, students review the word "mood." They then demonstrate their understanding by determining whether a situation would result in a good mood or a bad mood.

Put your finger under the first sentence.
Read the row with me. I want a cat. Mom said, "No cats!"
How does that make you feel?
Are you in a good mood? (no)
A bad mood? (yes) That's right!
Circle the sad face to show a bad mood.
Cross out the happy face.

Comprehension

Interactive Reading

"Research shows that teacher questioning strongly supports and advances students' learning from reading. Questions . . .
• give students a purpose for reading;
• focus students' attention on what they are to learn;
• help students to think actively as they read;
• encourage students to monitor their comprehension; and
• help students to review content and relate what they have learned to what they already know"
(Armbruster, Lehr, & Osborn, 2001, p. 54).

Research Snapshot

Fluency Foundations students comprehend on the go . . .

Students engage daily in interactive guided reading. As recommended by researchers, . . . discussions occur during reading when the ongoing process of guiding meaning takes place (Beck and McKeown, 2006, p. 23).

Gray text questions in the storybook:

• Increase active engagement during story reading

• Provide a framework for building story understanding

• Encourage students to use new vocabulary words

• Provide a scaffold to help students build inferences and draw conclusions

• Provide opportunities to develop and guide comprehension monitoring

IRMA THE DISCONTENTED COW

Chapter 1

I Wish I May, I Wish I Might

Irma the cow was an herbivore. To get enough food, she had to eat grass all day, day after day. Irma was a discontented herbivore.

What do you know about Irma?

Irma stood in deep green grass. She grumbled, "Graze, graze, graze! That is all I do all day long. I hate being an animal that eats only plants." Irma was discontented. That means that she was not happy with her life. 7 16 26 32 41

"Stop complaining," said the other cows. "We are lucky to be cows. We do not need to hunt for food. We graze all day on grass and weeds." 47 58 68 69

How does Irma feel? Why is Irma *discontented*?

50

PRIMING BACKGROUND KNOWLEDGE

USING VOCABULARY, DRAWING CONCLUSIONS

Research Snapshot

Building Knowledge

"From the earliest ages, reading is much more than decoding . . . If we want to raise later achievement and avoid the fourth-grade slump, we need to combine early instruction in the procedures of literacy with early instruction in the content of literacy, specifically: vocabulary, conventions of language, and knowledge of the world" (Chall & Jacobs, 2001, p. 21).

With *Fluency Foundations* units, comprehension building continues even as students work on reading fluency.

Fluency Foundations students:

- **Build background knowledge**
  The Song Contest—Students build background knowledge about herbivores, carnivores, and omnivores while being entertained by three animal contestants. Students have fun with repeated readings of their performances and also learn lessons about good sportsmanship.

- **Draw conclusions**
  Aesop's Fables—Students read adapted versions of Aesop's classic tales, and learn timeless lessons about hard work, persistence, ingenuity, and friendship.

- **Make connections**
  The New Bobcat—Students who have moved will identify with the main character, Rod, as he misses old friends and makes new friends.

- **Read multiple genres**
  Harriet Tubman Escapes To Freedom, Freedom Fighters—
  Read Well continues its commitment to a balanced instructional program—including multiple genres. This unit reviews lessons from *Read Well 1* as students read about Harriet Tubman's heroic flight to freedom and Martin Luther King's dream of freedom for all.

Fluency Foundations students build knowledge of the Earth we share.

Volcanoes on Earth

Students read basic Earth science information about volcanoes. Next, they learn how an ancient volcano erupted near Pompeii, sealing the people and land for 1,800 years. Finally, students read about the dramatic transformation of Mount St. Helens after it erupted in 1980.

From Seed to Flower

Students learn about the stages a plant goes through as it matures from seed to flower. In this life science selection, students learn about life cycles.

Nonfiction, Expository

Nonfiction, Expository

Fiction, Imaginative

And, read for fun!

Wacky Weather Facts

Students learn crazy weather facts through the fictional character Wiggy Weasel. Wiggy's motto is "a fact that is wacky keeps you happy." Wiggy reports on wacky weather such as a hailstone the size of a soccer ball and a shower of frogs that fell in England. This smart little weasel explains how these strange events happened.

Irma the Discontented Cow

Have fun with a discontented cow who wishes to be everything she is not. Through the magical power of a mighty bird, Irma the Cow gains first-hand experience as a carnivore and then as an omnivore. Find out with Irma which is best—being an herbivore, a carnivore, or an omnivore.

Fiction, Imaginative

Research Snapshot

Narrative Text Structure

During narratives, discussion questions direct children to the central content of the story, as recommended by Beck, Omanson, and McKeown (1982). Stories are then retold within a scaffolded story summary process. As students progress through the program, these strategies prepare children for written story mapping and retelling, which Baumann and Bergeron (1993) found to increase young children's comprehension.

Small steps . . .

Fluency Foundations **students read, comprehend, and work on carefully scaffolded written work.**

Skill Work

Students work on tool skills that are essential for crafting full written responses. These skills include handwriting fluency, word order, and spelling high-frequency irregular words.

Story Retells

Gray text story questions focus students on the important story elements, preparing students to write guided story maps and retells.

Written activities progress from:

- selecting statements that tell the beginning, middle, and end of a story to
- completing statements that retell a story

Comprehension Work

Comprehension activities gradually progress from simple multiple-choice formats to writing answers in a complete sentence. Students work on:

- defining and using vocabulary.
- reading and illustrating.
- identifying important story elements such as main character, goal, problem, action, and solution.
- identifying topics and important facts or details.
- predicting, explaining, and describing.

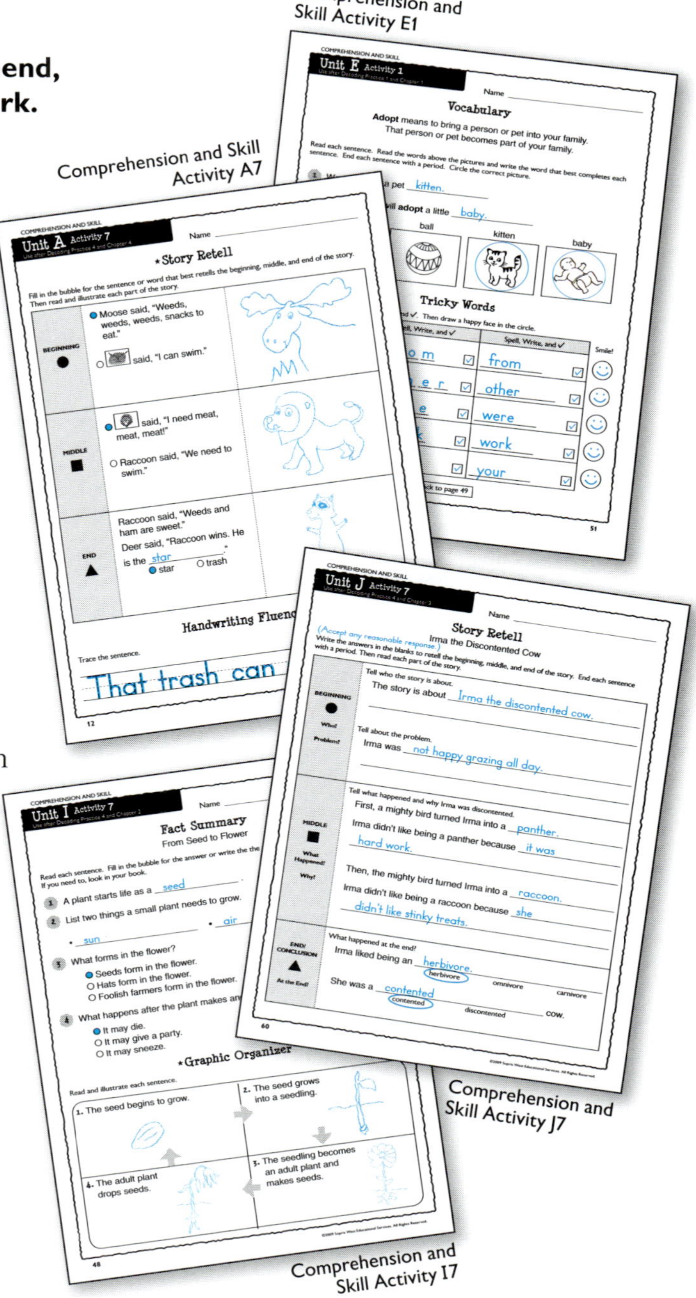

Comprehension and Skill Activity E1

Comprehension and Skill Activity A7

Comprehension and Skill Activity J7

Comprehension and Skill Activity I7

Fluency

Research Snapshot

Fluency

Reading fluency is recognized by researchers as an essential element of comprehension (Adams, 1990; National Reading Panel, 2000; Samuels & Flor, 1997). Hirsch (2003) explains, "A person who reads fast has 'automated' many of the underlying processes involved in reading and can, therefore, devote conscious attention to textual meaning rather than to the processes themselves" (p. 12).

Daily guided oral reading promotes fluency.

Guided Oral Reading with New Decodable Text

Each day, students read unpracticed text with the teacher. Guided oral reading affords the teacher the opportunity to focus students' attention on comprehension while simultaneously monitoring students' abilities to read unpracticed text with accuracy and expression.

After reading the selection, students practice any difficult words and reread.

Unit I, *Chaz and the Magic Beans*

Repeated Readings

Timed Reading

In Fluency Foundations, students do timed readings in most even-numbered story readings.

Short Passage Practice

In Fluency Foundations, students do Short Passage Practice in most odd-numbered story readings. In Short Passage Practice, the teacher provides explicit teaching of reading with ease and expression. The teacher explains how to read a passage, demonstrates, and guides practice by reading with students, then has individual students read.

Partner and/or Whisper Reading

Each day, students partner read or whisper read the day's story selection.

Daily Homework

In Fluency Foundations, students take home the day's story selection to read aloud with family members. Stories are reprinted on blackline masters for ease of home sharing.

Unit F, Teacher's Guide

STORY READING 1

STORY READING INSTRUCTIONS
The teacher reads the small text, and students read the large text. Read for accuracy first, then build expression and fluency.

COMPREHENSION PROCESSES
Remember, Understand, Apply

COMPREHENSION BUILDING: Discussion Questions and Teacher Think Alouds
• Ask questions and discuss text on the *first* reading.
• Encourage students to answer questions with complete sentences, when appropriate.
• If students have difficulty comprehending, explain your thinking or show them where the answer can be found in the text, then reread that portion of the story.

PROCEDURES
1. Story Introduction/Story Title: Building Knowledge
   Using Vocabulary

3. Repeated Readings
   a. Short Passage Practice
   Have students read the large student text. Do not reread the teacher text.
   • Demonstrate how to read a paragraph or two with expression. Read at a rate slightly faster than the students' rate. Say something like:
   Listen to me read the first paragraph. I'm going to pause at the end of each sentence.

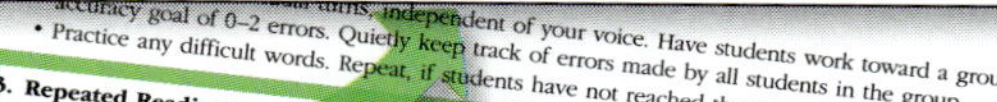

accuracy goal of 0–2 errors. Quietly keep track of errors made by all students in the group.
   • Practice any difficult words. Repeat, if students have not reached the accuracy goal.

3. Repeated Readings
   a. Short Passage Practice
   Have students read the large student text. Do not reread the teacher text.
   • Demonstrate how to read a paragraph or two with expression. Read at a rate slightly faster than the students' rate. Say something like:
   Listen to me read the first paragraph. I'm going to pause at the end of each sentence.
   When Harriet was little, she had to work hard. **Pause slightly between sentences.** She had to scrub and dust and could not rest. If she rested, she was hit.
   • Guide practice with your voice.
   • Provide individual turns while others track with their fingers and whisper read. Provide descriptive and positive feedback.
   [Cade], you did a great job. You paused at the end of each sentence.
   • Repeat with a second paragraph or two of student text.

   b. Partner Reading
   During students' daily independent work, have them do Partner Reading. Monitor and provide positive feedback as children practice.

   c. Homework 1
   Have students reread the story at home. (Story copies are available as blackline masters.)

210

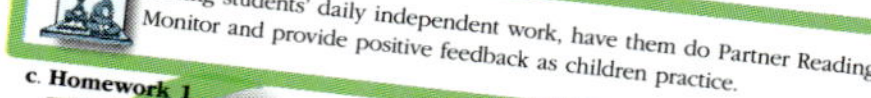

b. Partner Reading
During students' daily independent work, have them do Partner Reading. Monitor and provide positive feedback as children practice.

Practiced Passage

Harriet Tubman Escapes

Chapter 1 • Harriet's Dream

When Harriet was little, she had to work hard. She had to scrub and dust and could not rest. If she rested, she was hit. — 7, 15, 23, 25

Harriet said, "I am strong. I want to work with the men." She worked hard, but she wanted to be free. — 33, 40, 46

Harriet sang as she cut logs in the sun with the men. The sky and wind let Harriet feel free. — 54, 63, 66

She sang, "Let us go. Let us be free." — 74

Could Harriet be free? Could she run to freedom? — 75, 81

Harriet said, "I need to be free. I must try." — 84, 92, 94

Note: Numbers are for school use only.

Questions to talk about:
1. Who is the chapter about?
2. Describe the work that Harriet had to do.
3. What does Harriet want?

Unit D, Homework

Fluency

Research Snapshot

A Measure of Reading Competence

A wealth of research supports the value of oral reading fluency as an indicator of overall reading competence and its utility for helping teachers plan better instruction and effect superior student outcomes (Fuchs, Fuchs, Hops, & Jenkins, 2001, p. 252).

Fluency Lessons

In *Fluency Foundations*, each lesson is a fluency lesson.

Comprehension and Skill Work: Fluency Passages

In *Fluency Foundations*, most units also include special fluency activities—sentences or passages that provide students with an opportunity to build fluency with repeated readings, independent of the teacher.

Oral Reading Fluency Assessments

Because oral reading fluency is such a strong predictor of overall reading competence, each *Fluency Foundations* unit concludes with an oral reading fluency assessment. These assessments provide teachers with an ongoing tool to measure each student's growth in reading.

Unit F, Volcanoes on Earth

VOLCANOES ON EARTH

Chapter 1
Earth Has Layers

What is the story about? What do you already know about volcanoes?

Earth is the planet we live on. Scientists have learned many fascinating facts about Earth.

Earth has three layers. People live on the thin top layer. We call this layer the crust. — 8 — 17

The middle layer under the crust is called the mantle. Deep in the mantle is hot melted rock, or magma. — 25 — 34 — 37

The inner part under the mantle is called the core. — 45 — 47

Magma is found in pockets in the Earth's mantle.

Look at the picture. What part of the Earth do we live on? What is magma? Where is the hot rock, or magma?

6

Assessment, Unit F

UNIT F ORAL READING FLUENCY ASSESSMENT

ORAL READING FLUENCY PASSAGE

Camping in the Park

★My friends, my mother, and I went camping in the park. The park was a mix of green plants and forest. We visited the park in the spring. — 10 — 22 — 28

Mother had filled a box with food. We had lots and lots to eat. Then we ran and jumped on the great big hill. Matt said, "What if this hill was a volcano?" It was just a hill, but it was fun to play. — 39 — 52 — 65 — 72 — 82

Bill said, "Can you feel the Earth quiver and jiggle? Quick! Run!" We ran about until it was dark. — 91 — 101

Mother got a big quilt from the car, and we looked at the stars. What fun! I will remember this fantastic trip forever. — 111 — 114

Unit F, Comprehension and Skill Work

COMPREHENSION AND SKILL

Unit F Activity 5
Use after Decoding Practice 3 and Chapter 3

Name ________

Building Fluency

Passage Reading:
1. Read the story 2 times. Cross out a volcano each time you read the story.

A Volcano Erupts

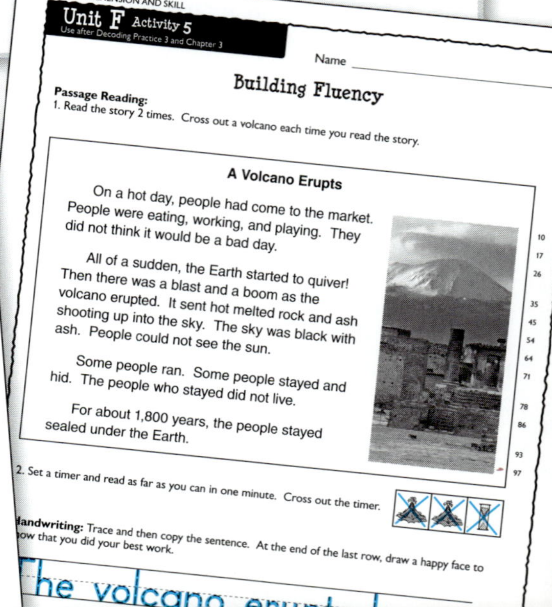

On a hot day, people had come to the market. People were eating, working, and playing. They did not think it would be a bad day. — 10 — 17 — 26

All of a sudden, the Earth started to quiver! Then there was a blast and a boom as the volcano erupted. It sent hot melted rock and ash shooting up into the sky. The sky was black with ash. People could not see the sun. — 35 — 45 — 54 — 64 — 71

Some people ran. Some people stayed and hid. The people who stayed did not live. — 78 — 86

For about 1,800 years, the people stayed sealed under the Earth. — 93 — 97

2. Set a timer and read as far as you can in one minute. Cross out the timer.

Handwriting: Trace and then copy the sentence. At the end of the last row, draw a happy face to show that you did your best work.

The volcano erupted.

ORAL READING FLUENCY

WCPM
PASS

Start timing at the ★ Mark errors. Make a single slash in the text (/) at 60 seconds. Have the student complete the passage. If the student completes the passage in less than 60 seconds, have the student go back to the ★ and continue reading. Make a double slash (//) in the text at 60 seconds.
Determine words correct per minute by subtracting errors from words read in 60 seconds.
The student scores no more than 2 errors on the first pass through the passage and reads 80 or more words correct per minute. Proceed to Unit G.
___ or more errors on the first pass through the passage and/or reads 79 or fewer words correct per minute, ... Unit F Extra Practice lessons, reteach and/or provide a ...

Phonics continues in *Read Well 2* and *Read Well 2 Plus*.

Read Well 2 and *Read Well 2 Plus* students enjoy expanding into popular trade books. Themes and topics address many content standards, such as geography, science and history. By the end of these programs, *Read Well* students can pick up and read just about any children's book that captures their fancy!

**Read Well 2 Skill Sequence and
Parallel *Read Well 1 Plus* Skill Sequence**

Read Well 2 Unit	Parallel *Read Well 1 Plus* Units	Sound Sequence Focus
1		Review
2	Unit 39	aw, re-
3	Unit 40	ew, ue, u_e, un-, ex-
4		Review
5	Unit 41	ow, o, -ful
6	Unit 42, 50	ge, -dge bi-
7	Unit 43	ci, ce de-
8	Unit 44	kn, ph, -able
9		Review
10	Unit 45	oa
11	Unit 46, 47	oi, ea i
12	Unit 48	gi, au be-
13	Unit 49, 50	oy -ous, dis-
14		-al, ible
15		-or, -ment
16		-ic, pre-
17		-ity, -sion
18		-ness, -less
19		in-, im-
20		

Read Well 1 Plus, Unit 46

Read Well 2, Unit 18

Read Well 2, Unit 12

Read Well 2, Unit 19

Read Well 1 Plus, Units 39–41

Read Well 2, Unit 21

Read Well 1 Plus, Units 47–48

Comprehension builds in *Read Well 2* and *Read Well 2 Plus*.

Guide students from learning to read to reading to learn.

Continue providing systematic and explicit instruction with *Read Well 1 Plus* or *Read Well 2*.

With *Red Well 1 Plus* and *Read Well 2*:

- address content standards in science, social studies, and health.
- build student vocabulary.
- develop a deeper understanding of multiple genres.
- develop comprehension strategies.
- have students write retells, fact summaries, reports, personal response journals.
- move students into trade books.

Read Well 2 and *Read Well 1 Plus* students finish these program reading sophisticated text in science, social studies, and history.

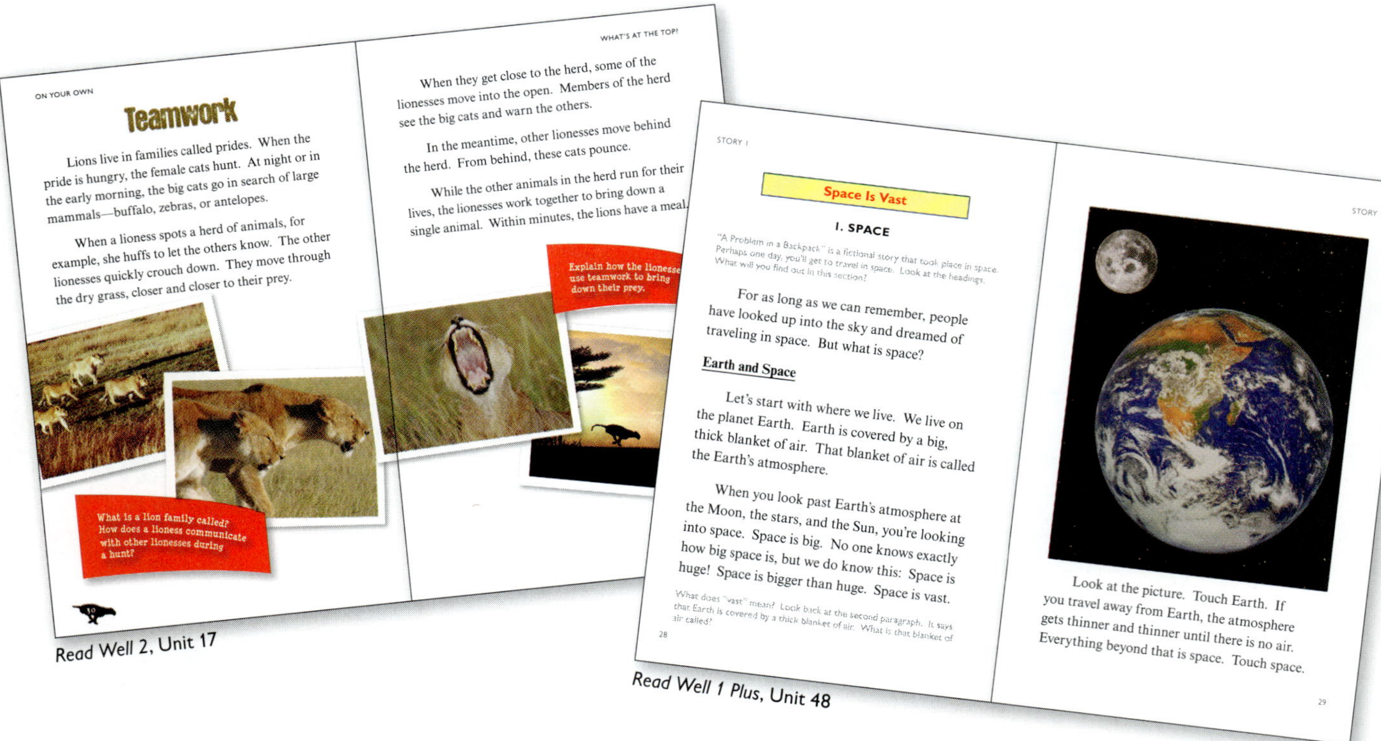

Read Well 2, Unit 17

Read Well 1 Plus, Unit 48

Your students will gain skills and strategies while being engaged, entertained, and of course, reading well.

Read Well's All-Inclusive Framework

Research Snapshot

Effective Reading Instruction for All

"The components of effective reading instruction are the same whether the focus is prevention or intervention: phonemic awareness and phonemic decoding skills, fluency in word recognition and text processing, construction of meaning, vocabulary, spelling, and writing.

"Findings from evidence-based research show there are dramatic reductions in the incidence of reading failure when explicit instruction in these components is provided by the classroom teacher.

"To address the needs of children most at risk of reading failure, the same instructional components are relevant, but they need to be made more explicit and comprehensive, more intensive, and more supportive in small-group or one-on-one formats.

"The argument is made that by coordinating research evidence from effective classroom reading instruction with effective small-group and one-on-one reading instruction, we can meet the literacy needs of all children" (Foorman & Torgesen, 2001).

Developmentally Appropriate

Position Statement

Developmentally Appropriate

". . . goals and expectations for young children's achievement in reading and writing should be developmentally appropriate, that is, challenging but achievable with sufficient adult support" (International Reading Association and the National Association for the Education of Young Children, 1985, p. 15).

Read Well is mastery based.

Appropriate Placement

Read Well students begin instruction with a small group placement that is appropriate to their instructional needs. Group placement is flexible and based on student performance data.

Continuous Progress Monitoring

The voices of individual children can be lost in a group, so it is important that all children have the opportunity to share their accomplishments one-to-one with supportive adults. Each student takes an individually administered assessment at the end of every unit to ensure that his or her needs are being met. When these assessments are used in combination with appropriate amounts of instruction and practice in *Read Well*, students are assured pre/post gains on external summative assessments.

Appropriate Pacing

Read Well's mastery-based, small group instruction allows each student to establish a critical primary reading foundation. Multiple entry points and varied lesson plans allow each child to progress at a pace appropriate to his or her development.

When implemented with fidelity:

- low-performing students can reach benchmark.
- average-performing students exceed expectations.
- high-performing students excel.

Challenging but Achievable

Learning should be as challenging for high-performing students as it is for low-performing students.

Because instruction in *Read Well* is explicit, many students master skills at a rapid pace. High performers excel rapidly and average performers often become high performers.

Watch them soar.

High-performing kindergarten students often complete *Read Well K* Unit 20 before the end of their kindergarten year. These students continue into *Read Well 1*. At the beginning of first grade, the children may place in *Read Well 1* Unit 30 and then progress into *Read Well 1 Plus*.

By second grade, these students are ready to place into *Read Well 2* at Unit 5 or higher. They will read to learn, write reports, and read trade books early in the school year.

Learning should be as easy for low-performing students as it is for high-performing students.

Watch them succeed.

Read Well's instructional design includes elegantly interwoven programs. The parallel scope and sequence of the *Read Well K–2* programs allows teachers to move students back and forth between components to achieve maximum results. Low-performing students do not need to be frustrated by multiple programs with different skill sequences. *Read Well* provides schools with what they need to collaboratively address the needs of those most at risk of reading failure.

Unique Instructional Design

Parallel Scope and Sequence

Read Well K

| Preludes A–F | Units 1–20 |

PARALLEL SKILLS TAUGHT IN:
- *Read Well K* Small Group, Units 1–20
- *Read Well 1*, Units 1–20

Read Well 1

| Intervention Preludes A, B | Units 1–20 | Units 21–38 | *RW1 Plus* Units 39–50 |

PARALLEL SKILLS TAUGHT IN:
- *Read Well 1 Plus*, Units 39–50 and
- *Read Well 2*, Units 1–12

PARALLEL SKILLS TAUGHT IN:
- *Read Well 1*, Units 16–38
- Reviewed in *Fluency Foundations*, Units A–J

Read Well 2

| *Fluency Foundations* Units A–J (Reviews *RW1* Units 16–38) | Units 1–12 | Units 13–20 | *RW2 Plus* Units 21–25 |

Fluency Foundations Materials

Getting Started: A Guide to Implementation

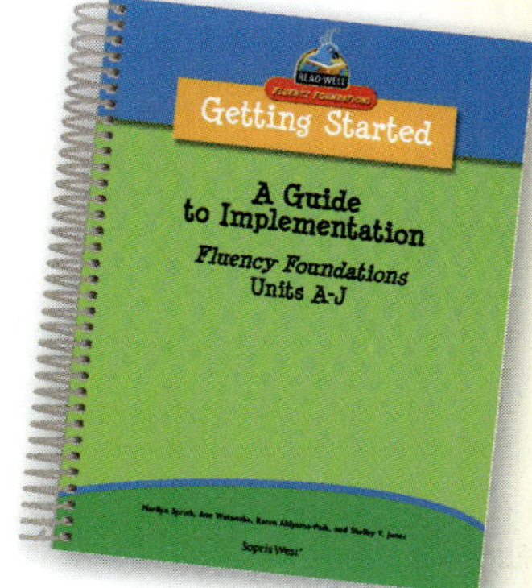

Includes:

- Program Overview
- Getting Started: Placing Students, Scheduling
- Small Group Lesson Planning
- How to Teach: Decoding Practice, Introductions, Story Reading
- Comprehension and Skill Work
- Homework
- End of the Unit: Assessments, Making Decisions, Extra Practice
- Blackline Masters: Timing Charts, Lesson Planner, Double Dose Lesson Planner, Placement Records, Assessment Records

Teacher's Guides

Two spiral-bound guides (Units A–E, F–J)

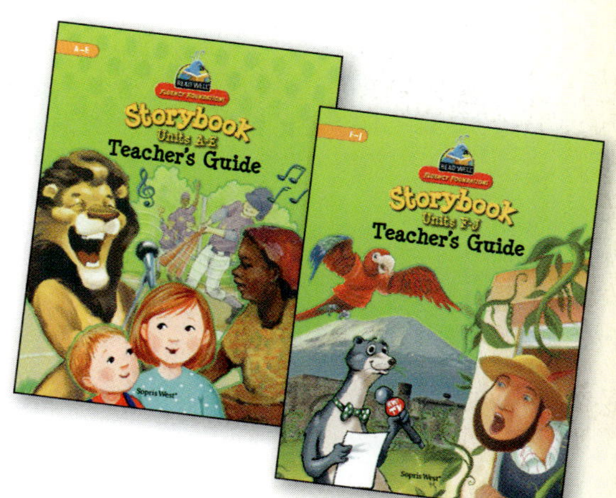

Includes:

- Important Tips
- Daily Lesson Planning
- Objectives
- Instructions: Decoding Practice, Story Reading, Comprehension and Skill Work

Sound Cards

Teaches and Supports:
Phonics

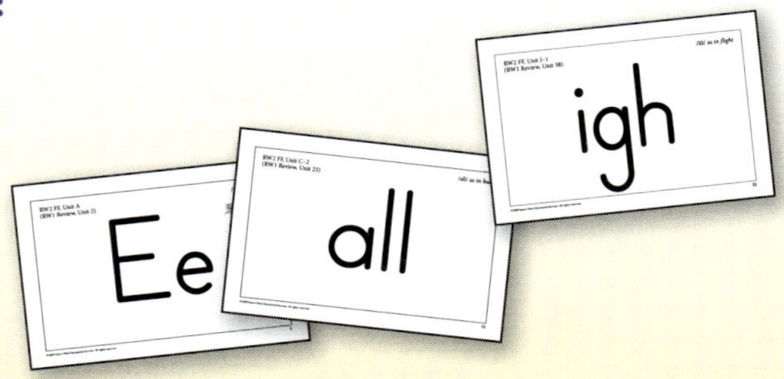

Materials

Student Storybooks A–E, F–J

(Nonconsumable)

Teaches and Supports:
Oral Language, Phonics, Vocabulary, Fluency, Comprehension

Student Activity Books A–E, F–J

(Consumable; blackline masters also included on the CD in plain and slanted text)

Teaches and Supports:
Oral Language, Phonics, Vocabulary, Fluency, and Comprehension. Includes: Decoding Practice and Comprehension and Skill Work

Extra Practice and Homework

(Consumables, blackline masters also included on the CD in plain and slanted text)

Teaches and Supports Extra Practice:
Phonics, Vocabulary, Fluency, Comprehension, and Home Connections

Teaches and Supports Homework:
Fluency, Comprehension, and Home Connections

Fluency Foundations CD at a Glance

The *Fluency Foundations* CD includes blackline masters for the following components:

- Decoding Practice
- Comprehension and Skill Work
- Homework
- Extra Practice
- Oral Reading Fluency Assessments
- Certificates of Achievement and Goal Setting
- Placement Records
- Assessment Records
- Jell-Well Planner

Getting Started

In this section:

2.1 Placing Students

2.2 Scheduling

APPROPRIATE PLACEMENT

As with all *Read Well* programs, *Fluency Foundations* is mastery-based. Success is predicated upon appropriate placement. To determine whether *Fluency Foundations* is appropriate, administer the *Read Well 2* Placement Test.

Placement Testing

Under ideal conditions, an assessment team composed of specialists and assistants completes placement testing during the first two weeks of school. Though placement results may reflect a summer of not reading, students should be placed in small groups during the second week of school. Group membership can change rapidly as students respond to instruction.

Materials Preparation

1. ***Read Well 2* Student Placement Test:** Make one copy of the Student Placement Test for each person administering the placement test (page 113).

2. ***Read Well 2* Student Placement Record:** Make one copy per student of the Student Placement Record (page 114). Keep the Student Placement Record in each student's file or portfolio as a pretest measure.

3. **Stop Watch:** Provide a stopwatch for each person administering the *Read Well 2* Placement Test.

Diagnostic Scoring

Administering the Placement Test

1. **Individually Administered:** Assess each student individually at a desk.

2. **Warm-up:** As a warm-up, have the student point to and read each Tricky Word. Mark errors but do not include them in the score. Have the student read the title and predict what the passage will be about.

3. **Timing:** Start timing the passage at the ★. Mark errors using the diagnostic scoring on page 30. Have the student complete the passage and continue reading for a full 60 seconds.

   - If the student has not completed the passage by the end of 60 seconds, make a single slash (/) after the last word read by the student, then have the student finish reading the passage.

   - If the student finishes the passage before 60 seconds have passed, have the student go back to the ★ and keep reading. Stop the student at 60 seconds and make a double slash (//) after the last word read by the student. On the second pass, mark errors differently (e.g., ✔).

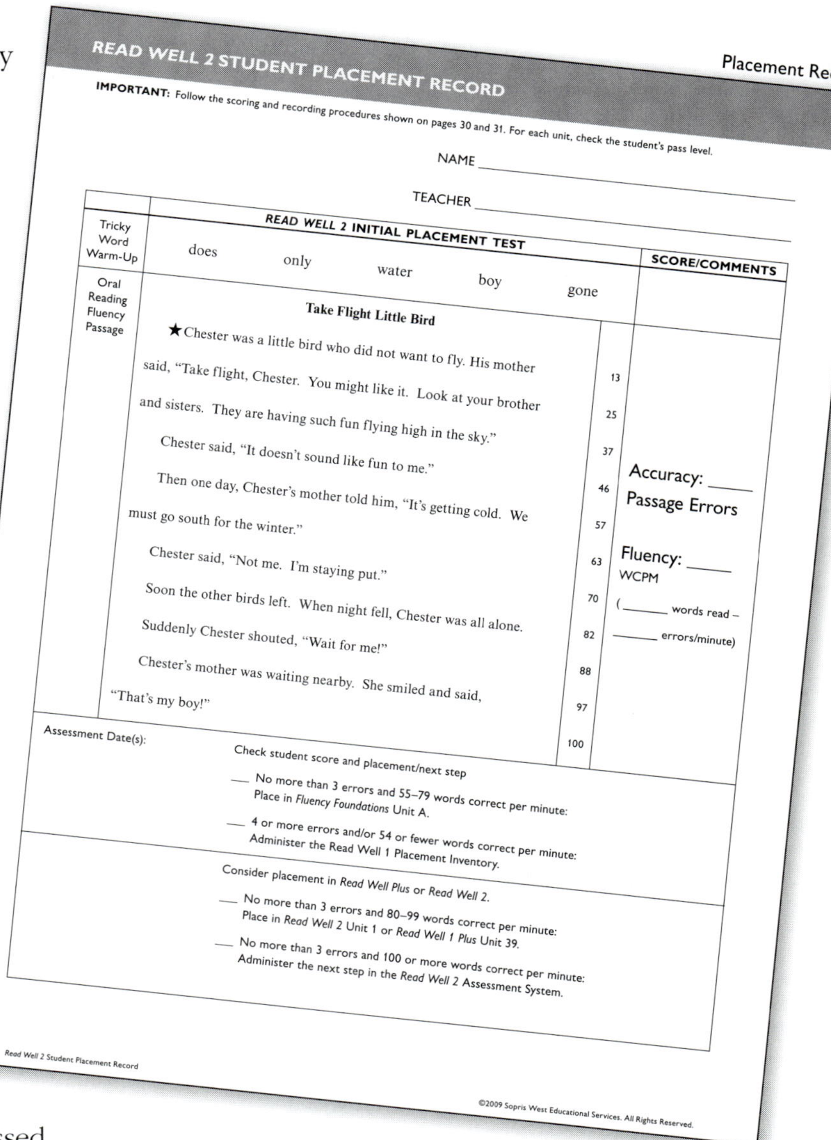

Diagnostic Scoring

If the student . . .	Then . . .	Record . . .
Needs Assistance	Wait three seconds. Gently tell the student the correct response, draw a line through the item, and write "A" for "assisted." Score as an incorrect response.	**Incorrect** A We could hear my kitten cry.
Mispronounces or Substitutes a Word or Sound	Draw a line through the word. Record what the student said. Score as an incorrect response.	**Incorrect** that Where was the kitten?
Omits a Word or Word Part	Circle the omission. Score as an incorrect response.	**Incorrect** The (sad) kitten was in the tree.
Inserts a Word	Write what the student said, using a caret to show where the student inserted the word. Score as incorrect.	**Incorrect** up Why was she there? ^
Self-Corrects	If the student spontaneously self-corrects, write "SC" and score as a correct response. If the student requires more than two attempts, score as an incorrect response.	**Correct** sc went/met We met at noon. **Incorrect** went/were/met We met at noon.
Repeats a Word	Underline repeated words. Score as a correct response.	**Correct** What could she do?
Reverses Words	Draw a line around the words as shown. Score as a correct response.	**Correct** She could rest.

SECOND TIME THROUGH		
Any Error	Make a √ over each word.	✔ Where was the kitten?

Determining Accuracy and Oral Reading Fluency Scores

1. **Accuracy Score:** Count the number of errors made in the passage.

   - If the student required more than 60 seconds to complete the passage, count the errors for the whole passage.

   - If the student read the passage more than once, count the errors only for the first time through.

2. **Oral Reading Fluency Score**: Count the number of words read to the double or single slash. Subtract errors made during the 60-second reading.

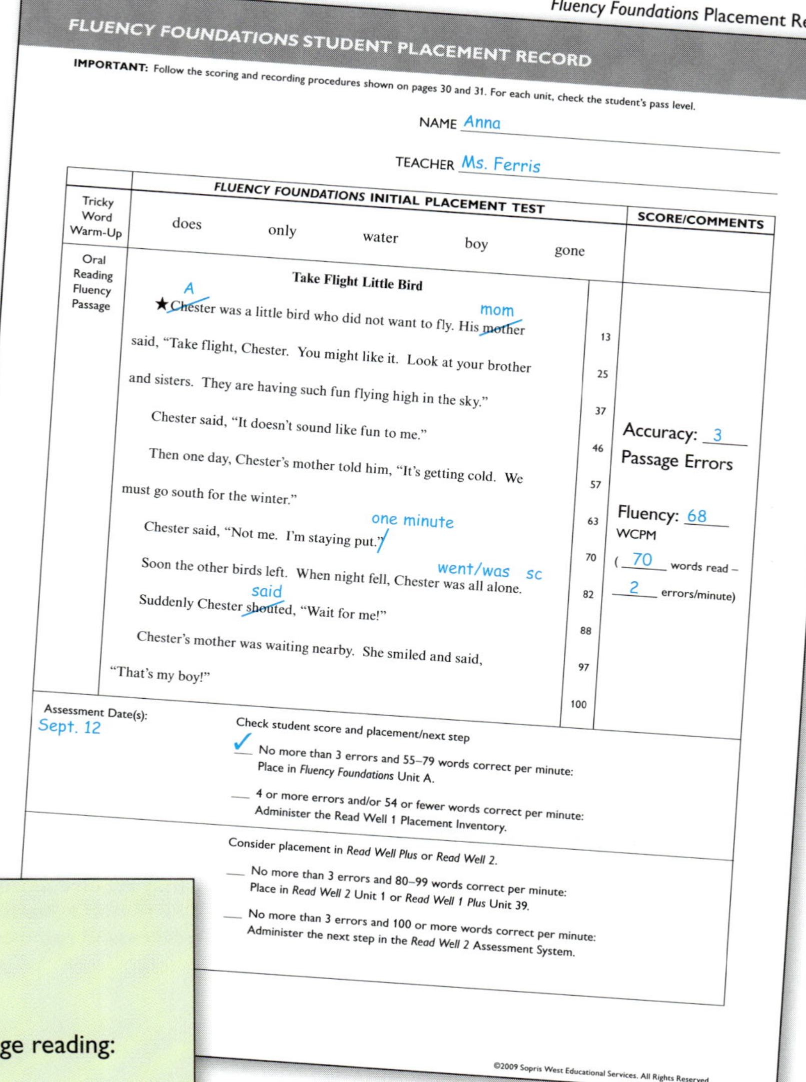

DETERMINING PLACEMENT

ANNA'S SCORE

Accuracy

Anna made 3 errors on the entire passage reading: Chester, mother, shouted.

Fluency

Anna read to the word "put" in one minute (/). During the minute she made two errors: Chester, mother. Anna read 70 words in one minute minus two errors. Thus, her fluency score is 68 WCPM.

Anna completed *Read Well 1* in first grade. Her scores in the last two units (Units 37 and 38) were weak, but with the year wrapping up the first grade teacher did not have an opportunity to reteach. Over the summer Anna has not read. *Fluency Foundations* will provide Anna an opportunity to master previously learned skills before moving on to new skills.

Diagnostic Scoring

Administration and Placement Schedule

The chart below summarizes the criteria for placing students in *Fluency Foundations*. Recommendations are included for placing students in alternative programs should student skill levels be too high or too low for this mastery-based program.

Administer	If the student scores . . .	Then . . . (2nd Grade)	Then . . . (3rd Grade)
Read Well 2 Placement Test	54 or fewer WCPM	• Administer the *Read Well 1* Placement Inventory.*	• Administer the *Read Well 1* Placement Inventory.*
	55–79 WCPM (0–3 errors)	Place in *Fluency Foundations* Unit A.	Place in *Fluency Foundations* Unit A.
	55–79 WCPM (4 or more errors)	• Administer the *Read Well 1* Placement Inventory.*	• Administer the *Read Well 1* Placement Inventory.*
	80–99 WCPM (0–3 errors)	• Place in *Read Well 2* Unit 1.	• Place in *Read Well Plus* or • *Read Well 2* Unit 1.**
	80–99 WCPM (4 or more errors)	Place in *Fluency Foundations* Unit A.	Place in *Fluency Foundations* Unit A.
	100 or more WCPM (0–3 errors)	• Administer the *Read Well 2* Unit 7 Placement Test.	• Administer the *Read Well 2* Unit 7 Placement Test.
	100 or more WCPM (4 or more errors)	• Place in *Read Well 2* Unit 1.	• Place in *Read Well Plus* or • *Read Well 2* Unit 1.**

*** See the *Read Well 1 Assessment Manual*.**

**** *Read Well 1 Plus* (Units 39–50) and *Read Well 2* Units 1–12 share the same phonics skill sequence. As a core program, *Read Well 2* has a broader range of objectives than *Read Well 1 Plus*. *Read Well 2* includes the introduction of more vocabulary and a wider array of writing and comprehension activities. The richer units in *Read Well 2* Units 1–12 may require more instructional time than *Read Well 1 Plus* to reach the same level of reading fluency. If *Read Well 1 Plus* is used for third grade intervention, students will be ready for *Read Well 2* Unit 13 upon successful completion.**

Scheduling

Adequate Instructional Time

To provide children with excellence in reading education, three variables are needed:

- A well-designed research-based curriculum (see Section 1)
- Adequate instructional time
- Skilled and caring teachers

This section addresses the second variable—instructional time requirements and scheduling scenarios.

**The more instruction and practice children receive,
the faster they will achieve mastery.**

Adequate instructional time is crucial. Time requirements for *Read Well* instruction include:

- five days of small group instruction per week for all students.
- a *minimum* of 45 minutes of teacher-directed instruction for each small group each day.
- a second dose of *Read Well* instruction for students at risk of reading failure.

Placement

Placement testing should be scheduled for the first and second weeks of school. Appropriate placement is necessary for children to benefit from *Read Well's* tailored instruction.

Collaboration

Think creatively. Be flexible. Work together.

When reading is a priority, schoolwide collaboration makes it possible to schedule adequate instructional time for developmentally appropriate groups.

Many scheduling variations are possible, each presenting flexible options. Sample schedules follow.

Scheduling Scenarios

2nd Grade *Read Well* Adoption • Instructional Collaboration With Regrouping Across Classrooms

SCENARIO 1: 90- and 60-minute *Walk-To-Read, One Group Per Teacher

Read Well works best with staff collaboration and regrouping across classrooms. The 90-minute Walk-to-Read model (5 days per week, 90 minutes per day) maximizes time students are academically engaged. Groups can be taught by classroom teachers, special education teachers, Title I teachers, supervised assistants, and other staff members.

This first 90-minute Walk-to-Read scenario shows three second grade homerooms and seven instructors available. The schedule below would be repeated in two other classrooms with Groups D, E, F, and G. Each teacher/assistant would teach one group during the 90-minute reading block.

Note: Spelling may be taught within the 90-minute block, and Composition is taught outside of the 90-minute block.

90-Minute Walk-to-Read (one small group per teacher/assistant)			
	Teacher 1 • Group A	**Teacher 2 • Group B**	**Teacher 3 • Group C**
10:00–10:15 (15–20 min)	**Teacher-Directed** *Fluency Foundations* Decoding Practice	**Teacher-Directed** *Read Well* Decoding Exercise	**Teacher-Directed** *Read Well* Decoding Exercise
10:15–10:40 (20–25 min)	**Teacher-Directed** • *Fluency Foundations* Story Reading • *Fluency Foundations* Comprehension & Skill Work (guided practice)	**Teacher-Directed** • *Read Well* Story Reading • *Read Well* Comprehension & Skill Work (guided practice)	**Teacher-Directed** • *Read Well* Story Reading • *Read Well* Comprehension & Skill Work (guided practice)
10:40–11:00 (15–20 min)	**Independent Work** • *Fluency Foundations* Partner or Whisper Reading • *Fluency Foundations* Comprehension & Skill Work The teacher monitors all students and provides additional instruction and practice for students who need assistance.	**Independent Work** • *Read Well* Partner or Whisper Reading • *Read Well* Comprehension & Skill Work The teacher monitors all students and provides additional instruction and practice for students who need assistance.	**Independent Work** • *Read Well* Partner or Whisper Reading • *Read Well* Comprehension & Skill Work The teacher monitors all students and provides additional instruction and practice for students who need assistance.
11:00–11:30 (30 min)	**Teacher/Assistant Directed** *Spelling & Writing Conventions*	**Teacher/Assistant Directed** *Spelling & Writing Conventions*	**Teacher/Assistant Directed** *Spelling & Writing Conventions*

60-MINUTE WALK-TO-READ

With less time, teachers teach spelling to the whole class.

*** With a Walk-to-Read schedule, teachers regroup across classrooms. The number of groups varies by the number of available instructors. (Groups are flexible in that students are regrouped frequently based on skill acquisition.)**

Scheduling Scenarios

3rd Grade Core Replacement • Instructional Collaboration With Regrouping Across Classrooms

SCENARIO 1: 90- and 60-minute Walk-to-Read, One Group Per Teacher

In the following 90-minute Walk-to-Read model (5 days per week, 90 minutes per day), students who place appropriately receive *Fluency Foundations* instruction as a core replacement program.

Note: Students start in *Fluency Foundations* and proceed into *Read Well 1 Plus*.

90-Minute Walk-to-Read (one small group per teacher/assistant)			
	Teacher 1 • Group A	**Teacher 2 • Group B**	**Teacher 3 • Group C**
10:00–10:15 (15–20 min)	**Teacher-Directed** *Fluency Foundations* Decoding Practice	3rd Grade Reading Program	3rd Grade Reading Program
10:15–10:40 (20–25 min)	**Teacher-Directed** • *Fluency Foundations* Story Reading • *Fluency Foundations* Comprehension & Skill Work (guided practice)		
10:40–11:00 (15–20 min)	**Independent Work** • *Fluency Foundations* Partner or Whisper Reading • *Fluency Foundations* Comprehension & Skill Work The teacher monitors all students and provides additional instruction and practice for students who need assistance.		
11:00–11:30 (30 min)	**Teacher/Assistant Directed** *Spelling & Writing Conventions*	**Teacher/Assistant Directed** *Spelling*	**Teacher/Assistant Directed** *Spelling*

60-MINUTE WALK-TO-READ

With less time, teachers teach spelling to the whole class.

* **With a Walk-to-Read schedule, teachers regroup across classrooms. The number of groups varies by the number of available instructors. (Groups are flexible in that students are regrouped frequently based on skill acquisition.)**

Double Dosing

To maximize progress, a second dose of *Fluency Foundations* instruction in the afternoon can provide high-risk students with the gift of time. The more time afforded in *Read Well* instruction, the faster students can attain mastery.

Supplemental Instruction With Fluency Foundations

Fluency Foundations can be used in many ways in multiple settings.

Summer School, Before Second Grade

Purpose: Preventing failure

Fluency Foundations can be used to give students who have acquired but not mastered first grade skills a boost in skills before second grade commences. The best time for instruction is four to six weeks before the school year starts.

If time allocated is	Then provide instruction and practice with . . .
30 mins	Decoding Practice, Story Reading
45 mins	Decoding Practice, Story Reading, Comprehension and Skill Work
60 mins	Decoding Practice, Story Reading, Comprehension and Skill Work, Repeated Readings
70–90 mins	Decoding Practice, Story Reading, Comprehension and Skill Work, Repeated Readings, Spelling and/or Extra Practice

Summer School, After Second Grade and Before Third Grade
Pull Outs or After School Programs, Second or Third Grade

Purpose: Intervention/Remediation

Fluency Foundations has the greatest potential for accelerating learning and preventing the confusion of a dual skill sequence when used as a core replacement program with a double dose in the afternoon.

Read Well can be used as an effective tutorial or small group intervention when a core replacement with a double dose of _Read Well_ instruction is not an option. _Read Well_ has been validated when used for supplementary instruction. See Denton, Anthony, Parker and Hasbrouck (2004).

If time allocated is	Then provide instruction and practice with . . .
30 mins	Decoding Practice, Story Reading
45 mins	Decoding Practice, Story Reading, Comprehension and Skill Work
60 mins	Decoding Practice, Story Reading, Comprehension and Skill Work, Repeated Readings
70–90 mins	Decoding Practice, Story Reading, Comprehension and Skill Work, Repeated Readings, Spelling and/or Extra Practice

Small Group Lesson Planning

In this section:

3.1 Daily Lesson Planning

3.2 Pacing

3.3 Sample Lesson Planning

3.4 Double Dosing

Daily Lesson Planning

Balanced Daily Lesson

Time is a precious resource.

Each day, all *Read Well* groups receive a balanced routine that purposefully integrates phonological awareness, phonics, vocabulary, comprehension, and fluency building.

Daily Lesson		
Teacher-Directed 45 minutes		**Independent** Teacher-Directed, as needed
Part 1	**Part 2**	**Part 3**
(Phonological Awareness, Phonics, Fluency, Comprehension) 15–20 minutes	(Vocabulary, Comprehension, Fluency) 20–25 minutes	(Vocabulary, Comprehension, Fluency) 15–20 minutes
• Decoding Practice	• Unit and/or Story Opener • Interactive Story Reading • Short Passage Practice • Timed Readings	• Story Reading With Partner or Whisper Reading • Comprehension and Skill Activities

Differentiated Plans

Similar to a budding long-distance runner or young pianist, the more instruction and practice young readers engage in—both across the week and each day—the faster they learn skills. When daily lesson periods are shorter, unit mastery takes longer. Progress is determined by:

- the learning needs of the children.
- the amount of practice each day and across the week.

Most of the teacher's guides include multiple lesson plans. The plans provide varied amounts of practice based on the students' skill level and response to instruction.

Fluency Foundations Plans

All *Fluency Foundations* units are 4-Day Plans. Four Extra Practice lessons are included in each unit for students who need additional practice. *Note:* If students require a 6- to 8-Day Plan to attain mastery, acceleration can be accomplished by scheduling a second dose of *Read Well* instruction during the day. (See pages 45 and 46 of this manual.) If students are accelerating, the 3-Day plan would be appropriate.

Core/Average 3- and 4-Day Plans

Most students will be able to complete a unit in three or four days.

3-DAY PLAN • *Acceleration*		
Day 1	**Day 2**	**Day 3**
• Unit Introduction	• Decoding Practice 2	• Decoding Practice 3
• Decoding Practice 1	• Story 2: The Song Contest, Ch. 2	• Stories 3, 4: The Song Contest, Ch. 3, 4
• Story 1: The Song Contest, Ch. 1	• Comprehension and Skill Activities 2, 3	• Teacher-Selected Comprehension and Skill Activities 4–7
• Comprehension and Skill Activity 1	• Homework 2	• Homework 3, 4
• Homework 1		

4-DAY PLAN • *Fluency Core*			
Day 1	**Day 2**	**Day 3**	**Day 4**
• Unit Introduction	• Decoding Practice 2	• Decoding Practice 3	• Decoding Practice 4
• Decoding Practice 1	• Story 2: The Song Contest, Ch. 2	• Story 3: The Song Contest, Ch. 3	• Story 4: The Song Contest, Ch. 4
• Story 1: The Song Contest, Ch. 1	• Comprehension and Skill Activities 2, 3	• Comprehension and Skill Activities 4, 5	• Comprehension and Skill Activities 6, 7
• Comprehension and Skill Activity 1	• Homework 2	• Homework 3	• Homework 4
• Homework 1			

Differentiated Plans

Fluency Foundations Plans (continued)

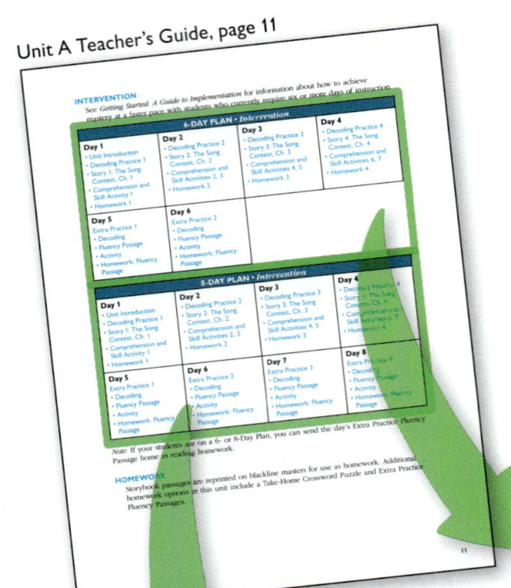

DOUBLE DOSING FOR PRE-INTERVENTION AND INTERVENTION

By double dosing high-risk readers, 8-Day Plans can sometimes be completed in four or five days without compromising mastery. (See pages 45 and 46 of this manual.)

Pre-Intervention

Divides single day reading and comprehension and skill across two days.

6-DAY PLAN • *Intervention*			
Day 1 • Unit Introduction • Decoding Practice 1 • Story 1: The Song Contest, Ch. 1 • Comprehension and Skill Activity 1 • Homework 1	**Day 2** • Decoding Practice 2 • Story 2: The Song Contest, Ch. 2 • Comprehension and Skill Activities 2, 3 • Homework 2	**Day 3** • Decoding Practice 3 • Story 3: The Song Contest, Ch. 3 • Comprehension and Skill Activities 4, 5 • Homework 3	**Day 4** • Decoding Practice 4 • Story 4: The Song Contest, Ch. 4 • Comprehension and Skill Activities 6, 7 • Homework 4
Day 5 Extra Practice 1 • Decoding • Fluency Passage • Activity • Homework: Fluency Passage	**Day 6** Extra Practice 2 • Decoding • Fluency Passage • Activity • Homework: Fluency Passage		

Intervention

8-DAY PLAN • *Intervention*			
Day 1 • Unit Introduction • Decoding Practice 1 • Story 1: The Song Contest, Ch. 1 • Comprehension and Skill Activity 1 • Homework 1	**Day 2** • Decoding Practice 2 • Story 2: The Song Contest, Ch. 2 • Comprehension and Skill Activities 2, 3 • Homework 2	**Day 3** • Decoding Practice 3 • Story 3: The Song Contest, Ch. 3 • Comprehension and Skill Activities 4, 5 • Homework 3	**Day 4** • Decoding Practice 4 • Story 4: The Song Contest, Ch. 4 • Comprehension and Skill Activities 6, 7 • Homework 4
Day 5 Extra Practice 1 • Decoding • Fluency Passage • Activity • Homework: Fluency Passage	**Day 6** Extra Practice 2 • Decoding • Fluency Passage • Activity • Homework: Fluency Passage	**Day 7** Extra Practice 3 • Decoding • Fluency Passage • Activity • Homework: Fluency Passage	**Day 8** Extra Practice 4 • Decoding • Fluency Passage • Activity • Homework: Fluency Passage

There is no substitute for time.

The amount of time required to master each unit of *Read Well* is dependent on: (a) the amount of time a school allocates to instruction, (b) the needs of the student, and (c) each teacher's skill and adherence to the program.

REMINDERS

- Teach your mastery-based groups five days per week, every week (with rare exceptions).

- Provide each group with a *minimum* of 45 minutes of uninterrupted teacher-guided instruction each day. Sixty minutes is adequate. With correlated spelling instruction, 90 minutes is optimum.

- Provide the lowest-performing third grade students with a second dose of *Read Well* instruction later in the day.

- Place students and begin instruction during the second week of school.

Pacing

Fluency Foundations Entry and Pacing Chart

The following chart shows the number of days required to complete units if groups pass Oral Reading Fluency Assessments on the core plan.

Fluency Foundations into *Read Well 2* • Second Grade Core and Third Grade Intervention
- The first shaded column shows the number of days per unit in the core plan.
- The second shaded column shows cumulative days of instruction for students who enter *Fluency Foundations* and proceed into *Read Well 2*.

Fluency Foundations into *Read Well 1 Plus* • Third Grade Intervention
- The first shaded column shows the number of days per unit in the core plan.
- The second shaded column shows cumulative days of instruction for students who enter *Fluency Foundations* and proceed into *Read Well 1 Plus*.

Fluency Foundations into Read Well 2
Recommended for second grade core, also appropriate for third grade intervention

RW2 Unit	Title	Days in Unit	Total Days
	First Week of School	4	4
	Fluency Foundations Units A–J	40	44
1	Maya and Ben	6	50
2	Mapping Our World	6	56
3	African Adventures	6	62
4	*Arthur's Pet Business*	2	64
5	Life as an Ant	6	70
6	Sir Henry	6	76
7	Stories From Hilo	6	82
8	Traditional Tales	7	89
9	Family Tales	6	95
10	Dino Discoveries	6	101
11	Dog Detective	6	107
12	*Magic Tree House: Dinosaurs Before Dark*	10	117
13	Spiders	8	125
14	Bats	6	131
15	Snapshots of the American West	6	137
16	Wild, Wild West	6	142
17	Science Digest Vol. 1: Food Chains	6	148
18	The Reef	6	152
19	*Flat Stanley*	7	159

Fluency Foundations into Read Well 1 Plus
Recommended for third grade intervention*

RW Plus Unit	Title	Days in Unit	Total Days
	First Week of School	4	4
	Fluency Foundations Units A–J	40	44
39	How the Chipmunk Got His Stripes	6	50
40	How the Camel Got His Hump	6	56
41	Why the Sloth Is Slow	6	62
42	Carlos the Curious	6	68
43	Maya the Magnificent	6	74
44	Nate the Great	6	80
45	A Class of Their Own	6	86
46	Frog and Toad Together	6	92
47	A Problem in a Backpack	6	98
48	Space Is Vast	6	104
49	Dinosaur Life	6	110
50	The Bobosaurus	6	116

After completing unit 50 in *RW 1 Plus*, test for placement in *Read Well 2* (projected placement Unit 13, Spiders) or assess for placement into a third grade program.

Sample Lesson Planning

Read Well lesson plans are easy to develop. Follow the plans provided in the teacher's guides.

Blackline masters of the lesson planning forms are found in the Appendix pages 111–112, and on the *Fluency Foundations* CD.

SAMPLE LESSON PLANNING FROM UNIT G • MR. DUSTRUDE

Mr. Dustrude is working with the 10 lowest-performing third grade students in his school. These students began with Unit A of *Fluency Foundations*. At the end of Unit G, Mr. Dustrude administers the Oral Reading Fluency Assessment. In this unit:

- a pass is 82 words correct per minute (WCPM).
- 6 of his 10 students read between 91 and 100 WCPM.
- 4 students barely pass with 82–83 WCPM.

Mr. Dustrude decides to go forward with the Unit G core plan—a 4-Day Plan. At the same time, Mr. Dustrude recognizes that to be successful, his lowest-performing students need more practice than the rest of the group.

Mr. Dustrude decides to adjust his time block by moving Partner Reading to the beginning of the reading period. While the group is doing Partner Reading, Mr. Dustrude will preteach the Decoding Practice to the four lowest-performing students. These four students will be given additional time at the end of each day to do more Partner Reading in their homeroom classes.

Mr. Dustrude also decides to try to find a way for the four lowest-performing students to receive a double dose of reading instruction. He explores the following possibilities for additional practice outside the reading block:

- Having his four lowest-performing students work with a second grade *Fluency Foundations* group as well as with his group
- Having an AmeriCorps volunteer work with each of the four students in Extra Practice tutorials
- Having a parent volunteer listen to each of the four students reread *Fluency Foundations* (or correlated *Read Well 1*) stories each day
- Having his two lowest-performing students work with the Special Education paraprofessional in *Read Well 1* in the afternoons

GROUP SKILL RANGE

When there is a range of skills in the group, those who need the most practice end up taking a back seat out of necessity. These students will need additional practice opportunities to remain successful and confident group participants.

Sample Lesson Planning

Mr. Dustrude's Lesson Planner for Unit G

1. Fill in the month, grade, instructor, and *Read Well* level at the top of the lesson planner.

2. For each day, fill in the date in the box in the upper left corner.

3. Select a plan from the unit lesson planning pages.

4. For each day, fill in the unit, Exercise numbers, Story Reading information, and Comprehension and Skill Activities.

5. Record any additional comments in the Notes column.

6. When teaching, check off what was completed. Adjust plans, as needed.

LESSON PLANNER   Month __October__   Grade __2__   Instructor: __Dustrude__   READ WELL __FF__

Monday	Tuesday	Wednesday	Thursday	Friday	Notes
10/3 Unit __G__	**10/4** Unit __G__	**10/5** Unit __G__	**10/6** Unit __G__	**10/7** Unit __H__	
✓ Decoding __1__ ✓ Story pgs. 16–17 ✓ Comp/Skill __1__ ✓ Partner Rdg ___ Assessment	✓ Decoding __2__ ✓ Story pgs. 18–19 ✓ Comp/Skill __2–3__ ✓ Partner Rdg ___ Assessment	✓ Decoding __3__ ✓ Story pgs. 20–21 ✓ Comp/Skill __4–5__ ✓ Partner Rdg ___ Assessment	✓ Decoding __4__ ✓ Story pgs. 22–23 ✓ Comp/Skill __6–7__ ✓ Partner Rdg ___ Assessment	✓ Decoding __1__ ✓ Story pgs. 26–27 ✓ Comp/Skill __1__ ✓ Partner Rdg ___ Assessment	**10/6** All students passed Unit G!
10/10 Unit __H__	**10/11** Unit __H__	**10/12** Unit __H__	**10/13** Unit __H__	**10/14** Unit __H__	
✓ Decoding __2__ ✓ Story pgs. 28–29 ✓ Comp/Skill __2–3__ ✓ Partner Rdg ___ Assessment	✓ Decoding __3__ ✓ Story pgs. 30–31 ✓ Comp/Skill __4–5__ ✓ Partner Rdg ___ Assessment	✓ Decoding __4__ ✓ Story pgs. 32–33 ✓ Comp/Skill __6–7__ ✓ Partner Rdg ✓ Assessment	✓ Decoding __1__ Extra Practice 1 ✓ Story __1__ ✓ Comp/Skill __1__ ✓ Partner Rdg ___ Assessment	✓ Decoding __2__ Extra Practice 2 ✓ Story __2__ ✓ Comp/Skill __2__ ✓ Partner Rdg ✓ Assessment	**10/12** Added Extra Practice 1–2. 4 out of 8 didn't pass. **10/14** All passed.
10/17 Unit __I__	**10/18** Unit __I__	**10/19** Unit __I__	**10/20** Unit __I__	**10/21** Unit __H__	
✓ Decoding __1__ ✓ Story pgs. 36–37 ✓ Comp/Skill __1__ ✓ Partner Rdg ___ Assessment	✓ Decoding __2__ ✓ Story pgs. 38–39 ✓ Comp/Skill __2–3__ ✓ Partner Rdg ___ Assessment	✓ Decoding __3__ ✓ Story pgs. 42–43 ✓ Comp/Skill __4–5__ ✓ Partner Rdg ___ Assessment	✓ Decoding __4__ ✓ Story pgs. 44–45 ✓ Comp/Skill __6–7__ ✓ Partner Rdg ___ Assessment	✓ Decoding __1__ Extra Practice 1 ✓ Story __1__ ✓ Comp/Skill __1__ ✓ Partner Rdg ___ Assessment	**10/20** Going to a 6-day plan for Unit I. Fluency scores not as strong.
10/24 Unit __I__	**10/25** Unit __J__	**10/26** Unit __J__	**10/27** Unit __J__	**10/28** Unit __J__	
✓ Decoding __2__ Extra Practice 2 ✓ Story __2__ ✓ Comp/Skill __2__ ✓ Partner Rdg ✓ Assessment	✓ Decoding __1__ ✓ Story pgs. 48–49 ✓ Comp/Skill __1__ ✓ Partner Rdg ___ Assessment	✓ Decoding __2__ ✓ Story pgs. 50–51 ✓ Comp/Skill __2–3__ ✓ Partner Rdg ✓ Assessment	✓ Decoding __3__ ✓ Story pgs. 52–53 ✓ Comp/Skill __4–5__ ✓ Partner Rdg ___ Assessment	✓ Decoding __5__ ✓ Story pgs. 54–55 ✓ Comp/Skill __6–7__ ✓ Partner Rdg ✓ Assessment	**10/24** Much better ORF scores. All passed. Will return to 4-day plan for Unit D. **10/28** All passed.

Double Dosing

Each year, in most classrooms, a few children need more intensive reading instruction than others. Early intervention is essential. The best way to maximize student progress is with a second dose of *Read Well*—typically administered by a Title I teacher, reading specialist, or an assistant. This second dose can be provided to a small group of students with similar needs or through one-to-one instruction.

THE BENEFITS OF A SECOND DOSE IN *READ WELL*

The second dose of reading is often given in the afternoon to distribute practice. Instruction may extend lessons or preview the next day's instruction.

Sample Scenarios

- A group of eight students splits into two groups—four students quickly master skills, but four students struggle. Rather than start another group and shorten daily lessons for each group, an assistant takes the lowest-performing students for a second dose of reading instruction each afternoon. Students reread that day's *Read Well* selection and preview the next day's Decoding Practice or Exercise.

- During a regular second dose of reading, the afternoon reading teacher repeats portions of the same lesson—allowing the group to build fluency and automaticity before moving to the next lesson.

- During a second dose of reading, the rest of the group goes ahead with the next lesson so the group can move forward faster.

- A group of low-performing students is scheduled for extra instruction, but only three days per week. Rather than share instruction in specific lessons, the interventionist teaches the unit's Extra Practice lessons. These parallel afternoon lessons help students build fluency without adding days to the unit.

- ELL students receive a second dose of instruction. The ELL teacher may choose to preteach the next day's story reading, review and preview Comprehension and Skill Activities, and/or provide extended practice with selected vocabulary words.

Note: With a double dose of reading instruction, low-performing students may achieve grade level reading expectations.

Sample Double Dosing Lesson Plan

This sample lesson plan is for a group of low-performing students who began third grade in *Fluency Foundations* as a core replacement program. Because this group started below grade level, the staff is working hard to help them catch up.

- Students in this group completed Unit E of *Fluency Foundations* with Passes on the assessment.
- With the support of the second daily dose, the teachers are following a 4-Day Plan. Each week is represented by two rows of instruction. With the double dose, teachers have built-in review with Extra Practice lessons. Without the double dose, students would require at least an 8- or 10-Day Plan.

DOUBLE DOSE LESSON PLANNER Month __October__ Grade __3__ Instructor: __Knapp__ READ WELL __FF__

Week 1

Teacher	Monday	Tuesday	Wednesday	Thursday	Friday	Notes
Knapp	10/3 Unit __D__ ✓ Decoding 1 ✓ Story pgs. 36–37 ✓ Comp/Skill 1 ✓ Partner Rdg ___ Assessment	10/4 Unit __D__ ✓ Decoding 2 ✓ Story pgs. 38–39 ✓ Comp/Skill 2–3 ✓ Partner Rdg ___ Assessment	10/5 Unit __D__ ✓ Decoding 3 ✓ Story pgs. 42–43 ✓ Comp/Skill 4–5 ✓ Partner Rdg ___ Assessment	10/6 Unit __D__ ✓ Decoding 4 ✓ Story pgs. 44–45 ✓ Comp/Skill ___ ✓ Partner Rdg ___ Assessment	10/7 Unit __E__ ✓ Decoding 1 ✓ Story pgs. 48–49 ✓ Comp/Skill 1 ✓ Partner Rdg ___ Assessment	10/3 Extra Practice for lowest 3 students with Mrs. Wong.
Wong	10/3 Unit D–EP1 ✓ Decoding 1 ✓ Story 1 ✓ Comp/Skill 1 ✓ Partner Rdg ___ Assessment	10/4 Unit D–EP2 ✓ Decoding 2 ✓ Story 2 ✓ Comp/Skill 2 ✓ Partner Rdg ___ Assessment	10/5 Unit D–EP3 ✓ Decoding 3 ✓ Story 3 ✓ Comp/Skill 3 ✓ Partner Rdg ___ Assessment	10/6 Unit D–EP4 ✓ Decoding 4 ✓ Story 4 ✓ Comp/Skill 4 ✓ Partner Rdg ___ Assessment	10/7 Unit D–EP1 ✓ Decoding 1 ✓ Story 1 ✓ Comp/Skill 1 ✓ Partner Rdg ___ Assessment	10/3 Continue with Extra Practice for these 3 students. Fluency is improving.

Week 2

Teacher	Monday	Tuesday	Wednesday	Thursday	Friday	Notes
Knapp	10/10 Unit __E__ ✓ Decoding 2 ✓ Story pgs. 50–51 ✓ Comp/Skill 2–3 ✓ Partner Rdg ___ Assessment	10/11 Unit __E__ ✓ Decoding 3 ✓ Story pgs. 54–55 ✓ Comp/Skill 4–5 ✓ Partner Rdg ___ Assessment	10/12 Unit __E__ ✓ Decoding 4 ✓ Story pgs. 54–55 ✓ Comp/Skill 6–7 ✓ Partner Rdg ✓ Assessment	10/13 Unit __F__ ✓ Decoding 1 ✓ Story pgs. 6–7 ✓ Comp/Skill 1 ✓ Partner Rdg ___ Assessment	10/14 Unit __F__ ✓ Decoding 2 ✓ Story pgs. 8–9 ✓ Comp/Skill 2–3 ✓ Partner Rdg ___ Assessment	10/12 All students passed.
Wong	10/10 Unit E–EP2 ✓ Decoding 2 ✓ Story 2 ✓ Comp/Skill 2 ✓ Partner Rdg ___ Assessment	10/11 Unit E–EP3 ✓ Decoding 3 ✓ Story 3 ✓ Comp/Skill 3 ✓ Partner Rdg ___ Assessment	10/12 Unit E–EP4 ✓ Decoding 4 ✓ Story 4 ✓ Comp/Skill 4 ✓ Partner Rdg ___ Assessment	10/13 Unit E–EP1 ✓ Decoding 1 ✓ Story ___ ✓ Comp/Skill 1 ✓ Partner Rdg ___ Assessment	10/14 Unit E–EP2 ✓ Decoding 2 ✓ Story 2 ✓ Comp/Skill 2 ___ Partner Rdg ___ Assessment	10/11 These students are also practicing the Unit E stories. Seem more confident.

REINFORCING INTERVENTION

When students are placed appropriately into *Fluency Foundations*, a second dose of *Fluency Foundations* instruction allows teachers and interventionists to provide students with intensive instruction that is coordinated and reinforces *Fluency Foundations* skills. Using a different supplementary program for intervention lessons can frustrate students if it requires them to learn an additional skill sequence.

How to Teach Decoding Practice

Read, practice, and teach well!

Read Well is a finely tuned instrument that is most effective in the hands of supportive, skilled, and well-trained teachers. *Read Well* provides the content and programming that allow you to concentrate fully on delivering instruction artfully, skillfully, and with enthusiasm.

Study the following section to learn how to teach the *Fluency Foundations* lessons skillfully and with confidence.

In this section:

4.1 **Preparing to Teach Decoding Practice**

4.2 **Letter/Sound Associations**

4.3 **Pattern Words**

4.4 **Multisyllabic Words**

4.5 **Tricky Words**

4.6 **Decoding Practice Summary**

Preparing to Teach Decoding Practice

Previewing Instruction

Each day, students complete a balanced daily lesson. This section will help you learn to teach *Fluency Foundations* Decoding Practice—Teacher-Directed Lesson Part 1.

Preview the Decoding Practice directions in the unit teacher's guide before teaching your small group. When teaching, simply follow the numbered tasks.

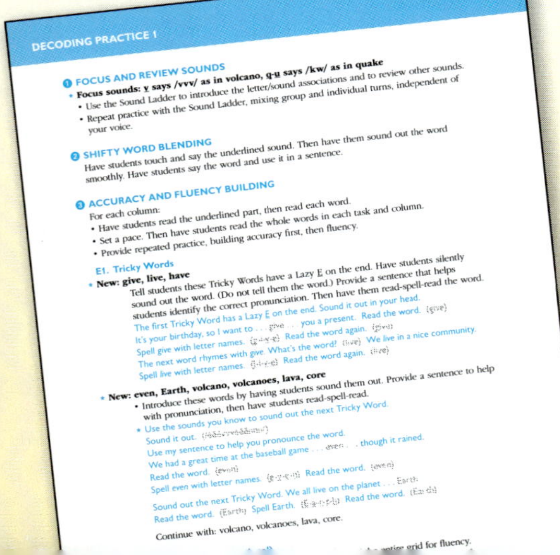

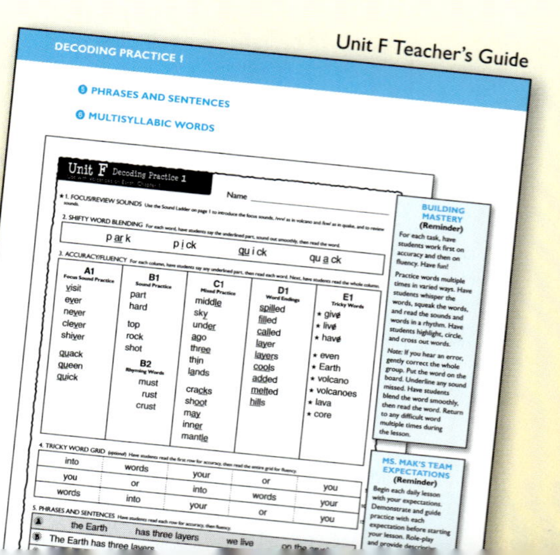

Scripting

Unique portions of the lesson are lightly scripted throughout the teacher's guides.

Teacher talk:
Blue text

Student responses with the teacher:
Gray text

Student responses without the teacher:
(Gray text in parentheses)

Word choices that can be tailored to the group or individual (names, objects, phrases):
[Bracketed text]

Letters that are referred to by name are underlined: a

DECODING PRACTICE 1

❶ FOCUS AND REVIEW SOUNDS

★ **Focus sound: o says /ŏŏŏ/ as in otter**
- Use the Sound Ladder to introduce the letter/sound association and to review other sounds.
- Repeat practice with the Sound Ladder, mixing group and individual turns, independent of your voice.

❷ SHIFTY WORD BLENDING
Have students touch and say the underlined sound, then sound out the word smoothly. Then have students say each word and use it in a sentence.

❸ ACCURACY AND FLUENCY BUILDING
For each column:
- Have students say any underlined part, then read each word.
- Set a pace. Then have students read the whole words in each task and column.
- Provide repeated practice, building accuracy first, then fluency.

C1. Rhyming Words
- Have students read the sets of rhyming words. Say something like:
  Everyone, what's the first word? (sand) The next word rhymes with *sand*. What's the word? (land)
- Have students identify what's the same about each set of rhyming words.
  What's the same about *sand* and *land*? (They both end with the little word *and*. They both end with a-n-d. They end the same.)

E1. Tricky Words
★ **New: looks, they, no**
- Introduce the new Tricky Words. Say something like:
  Your first new Tricky Word is *looks*. [Jorge] *looks* out the window. If we sounded it out, it would say /lŏŏks/.
  Mispronounce "looks" with the phonetic o-o as in moon sound.
  Do we say "He /lŏŏks/ out the window"? No, we say . . . looks.
  Read the word. (looks) Spell looks with letter names. (l-o-o-k-s) Read the word again. (looks)

  The next new Tricky Word is *they*. The girls went to the movie, but *they* will be back soon. Read the word. (they)
  Spell *they* with letter names. (t-h-e-y) Read the word again. (they)

  The next new Tricky Word is *no*. I have *no* sisters or brothers. Read the word. (no) Spell *no* with letter names. (n-o) Read the word again. (no)
- Have students read the remaining **review** words, building accuracy first, then fluency. Use the words in sentences, as needed.
- For any difficult words, have students read-spell-read the words.

❹ TRICKY WORD GRID (optional)
- Have students read the first row for accuracy, then read the entire grid for fluency.
- Once students are accurate, have individual students read for 30 seconds while other students finger track and whisper read. Calculate words correct per minute and record.

146   ★ = Introduction of a new/focus skill or activity

Unit C, Decoding Practice 1

Repetitive tasks, such as the daily Sound Review, are simply listed in the teacher's guides. Other tasks, such as morphographs and Tricky Words, are lightly scripted. Directions generally include bulleted instructions and any specific prompts that are needed to guide instruction.

Study and practice the following pages to learn how to present these tasks. With practice, instruction will become fluid and natural.

Principles of Explicit Instruction

When teaching, apply the principles of explicit instruction to attain high levels of student success.

HOW TO TEACH AND PRACTICE NEW AND DIFFICULT SKILLS

Demonstrate.

Show and model. Say something like: Listen. Watch. My turn.

Guide practice.

Practice the skill or strategy with students.
Say something like: Let's. Our turn.

Provide opportunities for independent practice.

Mix group and individual turns, independent of your voice.
Allow independence.
Say something like: All by yourselves. Your turn. I'll listen and watch.

Provide gentle, supportive corrections.

If students make an error or aren't sure of a response, it is an opportunity to learn.
Repeat steps: Demonstrate, guide practice, and mix group and individual turns, independent of your voice.
Practice other letter/sound associations, returning to any difficult skill until students respond correctly three times.

Acknowledge students' efforts and accomplishments.

HOW TO TEACH AND PRACTICE WORDS

Mix group and individual turns, independent of your voice.

With any known letter/sound associations, affixes, etc., start with independent practice. Do *not* demonstrate or guide.

Provide mastery-based instruction with supportive corrections.

Put the word on the board.

- Isolate the missed sound or syllable.
  Have students identify the missed element.

- Have students reread the word.

- Practice other words, returning to the difficult word until students respond correctly three times.

Acknowledge students' efforts.

> **NEW WORDS WITH KNOWN SOUNDS**
>
> With known sounds students have the skills to sound out new words, so do *not* demonstrate or guide. Begin with independent practice.

Managing Small Groups

Before you can effectively deliver instruction, it is important to teach students the behaviors that will make lessons both fun and productive. When behavioral expectations are clear, the focus can be on instruction. As with all classroom activities, begin by clearly identifying your expectations. What do you want your instruction to look and sound like?

WORKING IN SMALL GROUPS, ESTABLISHING EXPECTATIONS

Once students are in small groups:

- Teach your small group expectations with four or five positively stated rules.
- Demonstrate, as needed, and have children role-play each expectation.
- Have children verify their understanding of expectations.
- Provide ongoing positive and descriptive feedback.

Say something like:
We have four rules to remember. The first rule is to sit up. Everyone, show me how to sit up. Great job of sitting with your back to the chair. You are sitting second grade tall and ready to learn. Your next rule is to follow directions.

Let's see if you can follow directions. Simon says sit up second grade tall. Simon says touch your head. Simon says touch the words "*Read Well*" on the front of your Exercise or Decoding book. Great job! You know how to follow directions. I will expect you to follow directions during our group time.

TEAM EXPECTATIONS
1. Sit up.
2. Follow directions.
3. Help each other.
4. Work hard and have fun.

Your third rule is to help each other.
If [Ling] is needing help with reading a story, how can we help [her]?
(We can listen to [her] read. We can compliment [her] efforts.)
I am so glad you know how to help one another.
We are going to help each other try our hardest and do our best during group time.

The last rule is to work hard and have fun.
Do you know how to work hard? (yes)
Do you know how to have fun? (yes)
Wonderful! We are going to work hard and have fun.
That means we're going to stay focused, and we're also going to laugh when something is funny, and we're going to smile when we learn new things. Nod your head if you can work hard and have fun.

WORKING INDEPENDENTLY, ESTABLISHING EXPECTATIONS

If students are working independently while you are teaching groups, periodically scan the room. Acknowledge the efforts of students who are meeting expectations.

Letter/Sound Associations

Letter/Sound Associations, *Fluency Foundations*

Fluency Foundations reviews sounds taught in *Read Well 1* Units 1–15 and reintroduces letter/sound associations taught in *Read Well 1* Units 16–38.

Letter Sounds and Combinations
Cumulative Review of *Read Well 1* Sounds, Units 1–15
Ss, Ee, ee, Mm, Aa, Dd, Th/th, Nn, Tt, Ww, Ii, Hh, Cc, Rr, ea, Sh/sh, Kk, -ck

Unit A			Unit B	
oo /o͞o/ **Moon** Continuous Voiced (Long) *RW1 Unit 16*	**ar** /ar/ **Shark** Voiced (R-Controlled) *RW1 Unit 17*	**Wh/wh** /wh/ **Whale** Quick Voiced *RW1 Unit 18*	**Ee** /ēēē/ **Ed or Engine** Continuous Voiced (Short) *RW1 Unit 19*	**-y** /īīī/ **Fly** Continuous Voiced (Long) *RW1 Unit 20*

Unit B	Unit C			
Ll /lll/ **Letter** Continuous Voiced *RW1 Unit 21*	**Oo** /ŏŏŏ/ **Otter** Continuous Voiced (Short) *RW1 Unit 22*	**Bb** /b/ **Bat** Quick Voiced (not buh) *RW1 Unit 23*	**all** /all/ **Ball** Voiced *RW1 Unit 23*	**Gg** /g/ **Gorilla** Quick Voiced (not guh) *RW1 Unit 24*

Unit C	Unit D			Unit E
Ff /fff/ **Frog** Continuous Unvoiced *RW1 Unit 25*	**Uu** /ŭŭŭ/ **Umbrella** Continuous Voiced (Short) *RW1 Unit 26*	**er** /er/ **Sister** Voiced (R-Controlled) *RW1 Unit 27*	**oo** /o͝o/ **Book** Voiced (Short) *RW1 Unit 27*	**Aa** /ə/ **Ago** Voiced (Schwa) *RW1 Unit 28*

Unit E			Unit F	
Yy /y-/ **Yarn** Quick Voiced *RW1 Unit 28*	**Pp** /p/ **Pig** Quick Unvoiced (not puh) *RW1 Unit 29*	**ay** /āāā/ **Hay** Voiced *RW1 Unit 29*	**Vv** /vvv/ **Volcano** Continuous Voiced *RW1 Unit 30*	**Qu/qu** /kw/ **Quake** Quick Unvoiced *RW1 Unit 31*

Unit F			Unit G	
Jj /j/ **Jaguar** Quick Voiced (not juh) *RW1 Unit 32*	**or** /or/ **Horn** Voiced (R-Controlled) *RW1 Unit 33*	**Xx** /ksss/ **Fox** Continuous Unvoiced *RW1 Unit 33*	**a_e** /āāā/ **Cake** Bossy E Voiced (Long) *RW1 Unit 34*	**Zz** /zzz/ **Zebra** Continuous Voiced *RW1 Unit 34*

Unit G	Unit H			Unit I
-y /ēēē/ **Baby** Voiced *RW1 Unit 35*	**i_e** /īīī/ **Kite** Bossy E Voiced (Long) *RW1 Unit 35*	**ou** /ou/ **Cloud** Voiced *RW1 Unit 36*	**ow** /ou/ **Cow** Voiced *RW1 Unit 36*	**Ch/ch** /ch/ **Chicken** Quick Unvoiced *RW1 Unit 37*

Unit I		Unit J	
ai /āāā/ **Rain** Voiced (Long) *RW1 Unit 37*	**o_e** /ōōō/ **Bone** Bossy E Voiced (Long) *RW1 Unit 38*	**igh** /īīī/ **Flight** Voiced (Long) *RW1 Unit 38*	**ir** /ir/ **Bird** Voiced (R-Controlled) *RW1 Unit 38*

Fluency Foundations Sequence and Sound Pronunciation Guide

Sound Review

Each Decoding Practice in *Fluency Foundations* begins with a Sound Review. The daily Sound Review builds speed of sound recognition and facilitates easy, fluent word recognition.

Sound Reviews are often conducted using the Sound Cards. In Sound Reviews, students practice selected letter/sound combinations taught in previous units, as well as any new sounds previously introduced in the unit.

HOW TO BUILD FLUENCY WITH SOUND CARDS

- Demonstrate reading a few of the sounds at an appropriate pace. Say something like:
  You're going to read the sounds about this fast. /ā/, /ĭ/, /ā/ . . .

- Guide reading a few of the sounds at an appropriate pace. Say something like:
  Read the sounds with me. /ā/, /ĭ/, /ā/...

- Mix group and individual turns, independent of your voice. Say something like:
  I'm going to shuffle the cards again.
  Read the sounds without me. (/ē/, /ĭ/, /sh/, /wh/ . . .)
  [Maria], now it's your turn to read five sounds.

Have your partner make a mistake and then follow the steps in "Working Toward Mastery, Correcting Errors."

PRACTICE WITH A COLLEAGUE

To get ready for a Sound Review:

1. Study the script.
2. Practice the sounds with a colleague.
3. Use Sound Cards to practice teaching a Sound Review.

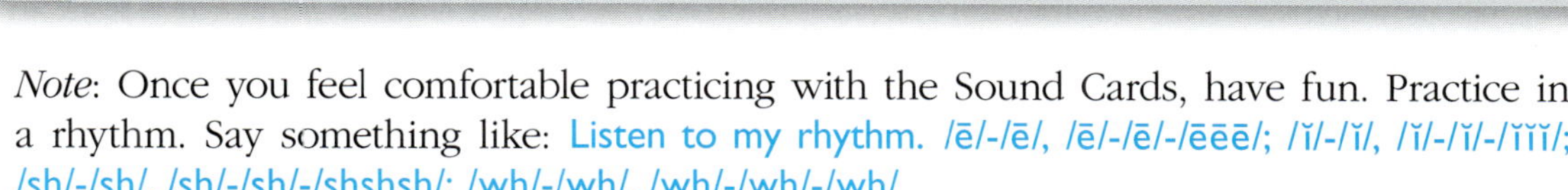

Note: Once you feel comfortable practicing with the Sound Cards, have fun. Practice in a rhythm. Say something like: Listen to my rhythm. /ē/-/ē/, /ē/-/ē/-/ēēē/; /ĭ/-/ĭ/, /ĭ/-/ĭ/-/ĭĭĭ/; /sh/-/sh/, /sh/-/sh/-/shshsh/; /wh/-/wh/, /wh/-/wh/-/wh/

Sound Review

WORKING TOWARD MASTERY, CORRECTING ERRORS

In this example, the student reads /āāā/ instead of /ăăă/.

- Gently correct the whole group. Clarify:
  Sometimes the letter <u>a</u> says its name.
  Demonstrate. The letter <u>a</u> also says /ăăă/ as in ant.
  Guide. Say the sound with me. /ăăă/
  Yes, /ăăă/ as in . . . ant.
  Guide. Say the sound with me three times.
  /ă/, /ă/, /ăăă/

- Provide practice, independent of your voice:
  Say the sound three times by yourselves.
  (/ă/, /ă/, /ăăă/)

- Provide discrimination practice by reinserting
  the card. Each time the difficult card comes up,
  prompt the correct sound. Practice until students
  read the sound correctly on three consecutive attempts.
  Read the sounds without me. (/ĭĭĭ/, /ēēē/, /ththth/)
  Here's the difficult sound. Remember to say the sound. (/ăăă/)
  You've got it. **Reinsert the difficult card.**
  Keep going. (/ĕĕĕ/, /o͞o/, /ar/, /ŭŭŭ/, /ăăă/)
  You got the hard sound two times. **Reinsert the difficult card.**
  Let's see if you can get it again. (/o͞o/, /or/, /ŭŭŭ/, /ăăă/)
  Excellent. You read the difficult sound /ăăă/ three times.
  It isn't difficult for you anymore.

PRACTICE WITH A COLLEAGUE

To practice correcting errors:

1. Study the script.
2. Practice the sounds with a colleague. Have your colleague make one or two errors.

Focus and Review Sounds, *Fluency Foundations*

Sound Ladder

In *Fluency Foundations*, each unit opens with a Sound Ladder activity. The Sound Ladder activity introduces the first letter/sound focus. Each new sound focus is introduced explicitly and includes a key word mnemonic.

HOW TO INTRODUCE FOCUS SOUNDS

- Introduce the focus sound.
  Everyone, touch under the picture of the otter at the bottom of the ladder. Did you know that o often says /ŏŏŏ/ as in otter? Everyone, say "o says /ŏŏŏ/ as in otter."
  (o says /ŏŏŏ/ as in otter)

- Set a pace and rhythm.
  Starting at the bottom of the ladder, you're going to read each rung like this: o as in otter, /ŏ/, /ŏ/, /ŏŏŏ/, l as in letter, /l/, /l/, /lll/; a-r as in shark, /ar/, /ar/, /ar/ . . .

- Have students read each rung of the ladder.
  Now it's your turn to read the ladder.
  Start at the bottom and keep going up.
  Put your finger under the otter and track with
  your finger as you move up the ladder.
  (o as in otter, /ŏ/, /ŏ/, /ŏŏŏ/, l as in letter, /l/, /l/, /lll/; a-r as in shark, /ar/, /ar/, /ar/ . . .)

- Repeat, using group and individual turns, on each rung of the ladder and on the whole ladder.
  Let's do that again. Listen carefully for your turn.
  Everyone . . . (o as in otter, /ŏ/, /ŏ/, /ŏŏŏ/, l as in letter, /l/, /l/, /lll/)
  [Nancy], next sound . . . (a-r as in shark, /ar/, /ar/, /ar/)
  [Joshua], next sound . . . (w-h as in whale, /wh/, /wh/, /wh/)

- Provide repeated practice to build fluency.
  Mix group and individual turns, independent of your voice.

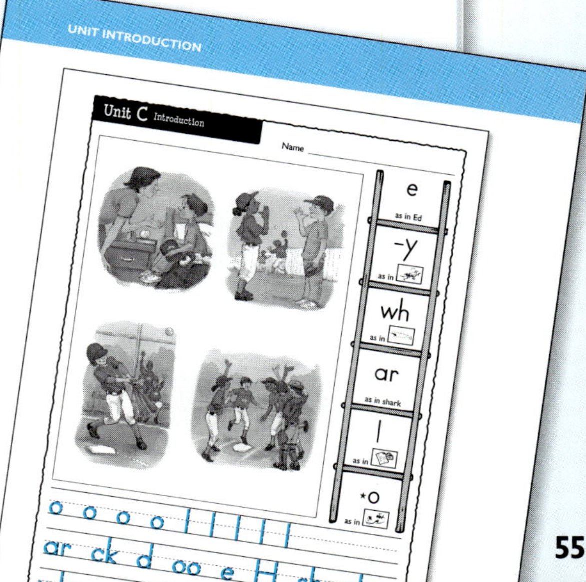

Pattern Words

Fluency Foundations Decoding Practice includes pattern word practice with Shifty Word Blending and Accuracy and Fluency Building tasks. These tasks help students:

- learn and/or maintain the skill of blending.
- review skills for maintenance and fluency.
- apply known skills to new words.
- practice new story words for fluent story reading.

Unit A, Decoding Practice 1

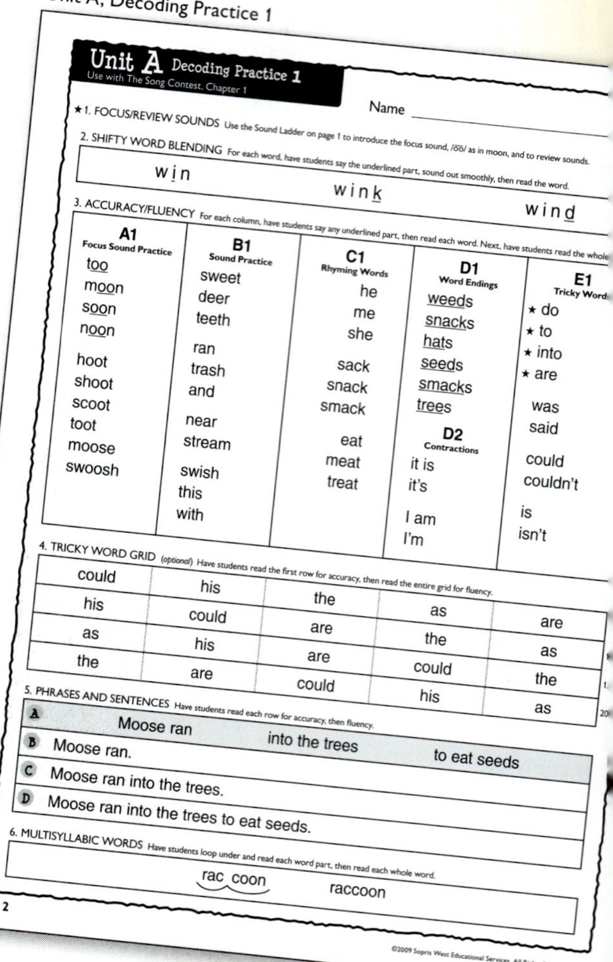

Unit A Decoding Practice 1
Use with The Song Contest, Chapter 1

Name ___________

★1. FOCUS/REVIEW SOUNDS Use the Sound Ladder on page 1 to introduce the focus sound, /oo/ as in moon, and to review sounds.

2. SHIFTY WORD BLENDING For each word, have students say the underlined part, sound out smoothly, then read the word.

w i n   w i n k   w i n d

3. ACCURACY/FLUENCY For each column, have students say any underlined part, then read each word. Next, have students read the whole

A1 Focus Sound Practice	B1 Sound Practice	C1 Rhyming Words	D1 Word Endings	E1 Tricky Words
too	sweet	he	weeds	★ do
moon	deer	me	snacks	★ to
soon	teeth	she	hats	★ into
noon	ran		seeds	★ are
hoot	trash	sack	smacks	
shoot	and	snack	trees	was
scoot	near	smack	**D2** Contractions	said
toot	stream	eat	it is	
moose	swish	meat	it's	could
swoosh	this	treat		couldn't
	with		I am	is
			I'm	isn't

4. TRICKY WORD GRID (optional) Have students read the first row for accuracy, then read the entire grid for fluency.

could	his	the	as	
his	could	are	the	are
as	his	are	could	as
the	are	could	his	the
				as

5. PHRASES AND SENTENCES Have students read each row for accuracy, then fluency.

A	Moose ran	into the trees	to eat seeds
B	Moose ran.		
C	Moose ran into the trees.		
D	Moose ran into the trees to eat seeds.		

6. MULTISYLLABIC WORDS Have students loop under and read each word part, then read each whole word.

rac coon   raccoon

2

Shifty Word Blending

Research Snapshot

Eye Movement Research

"Skillful readers visually process virtually every individual letter of every word they read, and this is true whether they are reading isolated words or meaningful, connected text" (Stahl, Osborn, & Lehr, 1990, p. 18).

If your students were in *Read Well K* and/or *Read Well 1*, they learned the research-based strategy of blending, or sounding out words. In *Fluency Foundations* this critical strategy is practiced in Shifty Word Blending. It is also used as a mastery-based correction procedure when students make errors.

Shifty Word Blending

In the Shifty Word exercises, students read the underlined sound(s), sound out the word *smoothly*, then read the word. This three-step process provides a reliable and efficient strategy for figuring out new and difficult words and pre-corrects common errors (e.g., reading "wen" for "win," "tin" for "ten," "lost" for "loss," "shout" for "spout").

Shifty Word Blending

TEACH EXPLICITLY

Demonstrate. Say something like:

> With Shifty Words, only one sound changes from word to word.
> Listen to me read the underlined sound in the first word. /ĭĭĭ/
> Now I'll sound out the whole word smoothly. /wwwĭĭĭnnn/
> The word is *win*. We can *win* the game.

Guide. Say something like:

> Touch the underlined sound in the first word and say the sound. /ĭĭĭ/
> Now sound out the word. /wwwĭĭĭnnn/ Read the word. (win)

Demonstrate and guide, as needed, for each remaining word.

For the remaining words, have students say the underlined part, sound out smoothly, then read the word. Use each word in a sentence.

Provide Practice, independent of your voice, as soon as students can be successful.

Shifty Word Blending, Correction Procedure

Errors create an opportunity for learning.

If students have difficulty, remember:
- Provide gentle group corrections.
- Provide diagnostic corrections.
- Then practice to mastery.

Word	Error	Correction
shark	Blends /shshshăăăk/ Misidentifies sound	Put the word on the board. Underline the missed letter/sound association. Have students correct the sound, then blend the word again. sh<u>ar</u>k Read the underlined sound. (/ar/) Sound it out smoothly. (/shshshark/) Read the word. (shark)
shark	Blends /sh/•/ark/ instead of /shshshark/ Fails to blend smoothly	Do discrimination training. (Have students identify whether you are doing Smooth Blending or Bumpy Blending—e.g., segmenting.) Listen to me: /sh/ • /ar/ • /k/ Was that smooth or bumpy? (bumpy) Bumpy Blending doesn't sound like reading, so it is important to sound out smoothly. Listen to me again. /shshshark/ Was that smooth or bumpy? (smooth) Now it's your turn. Sound out *shark* smoothly. (/shshshark/)

Three Consecutive Correct Responses
Once an immediate correction has been made, go on to other examples and return to the difficult word for three consecutive correct responses.

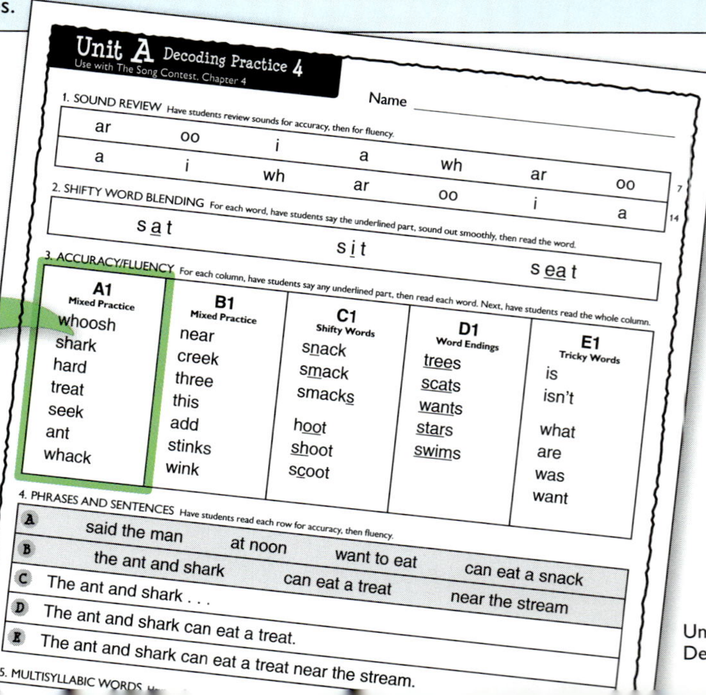

Shifty Word Blending, Correction Procedure

SMOOTH BLENDING CORRECTION

If students do not sound out smoothly:

- **Provide descriptive feedback.** Say something like:
  I heard Bumpy Blending: /wh/ • /ăăă/ • /k/.
  When we read, it sounds funny to do Bumpy Blending.
  Listen to this sentence: I can /wh/ • /ăăă/ • /k/ the ball.

- **Demonstrate** sounding out the word "whack" smoothly.
  If you sound out smoothly, your reading will sound like we talk.
  Listen to me sound out smoothly.
  I won't stop between the sounds. /whăăăk/
  Tell me the word. (whack)
  Listen: I can / whăăăk / the ball. What can I do? (whack the ball)

- **Guide.**
  Let's sound out smoothly. /whăăăk/ Tell me the word. (whack)

- **Repeat**, mixing group and individual turns, independent of your voice.
  Sound out smoothly by yourselves. (/whăăăk/)
  Tell me the word. (whack)

- **Practice** other examples. Return to the difficult word at least three times.

- **Acknowledge** students' efforts.

SOUND ERROR CORRECTION

If a student misidentifies a word, use the Shifty Word Blending procedure so students learn to apply the strategy of sounding out. Do not tell students the correct word. Write any missed word on a white board or paper.

Students read "fox" for "fix."

- Have students identify the missed sound.
  There was one sound that tricked some of us.
  Point to the sound. Tell me the sound. (/ĭĭĭ/)

- Have students sound out the word with the correct sound.
  Sound out the word smoothly. (/fffĭĭĭksss/)
  Read the word. (fix) The car is broken. We need to . . . (fix it).
  That's right. We wouldn't fox a car, but we would . . . fix it.

- Practice other words.

- Return to the difficult word at least three times.

- Acknowledge students' efforts.
  Great! You know the difference between fox and fix.

Accuracy and Fluency Building

General Procedures

A variety of tasks provide practice with letter/sound associations in words. These tasks often appear in the Accuracy and Fluency columns. Specific instructions and sample scripts for new and difficult tasks are provided in the teacher's guides. Review the scripts provided before instruction. During instruction, keep your focus on the students.

Remember, the scripts are provided so you can prepare for instruction by visualizing a lesson.

Steps for Accuracy and Fluency Building are included on each Exercise as a quick guide to instruction.

The teacher's guides include sentence suggestions to help students make language connections after they have decoded individual words.

The teacher's guides include specific instructions and sample scripts for new and difficult tasks.

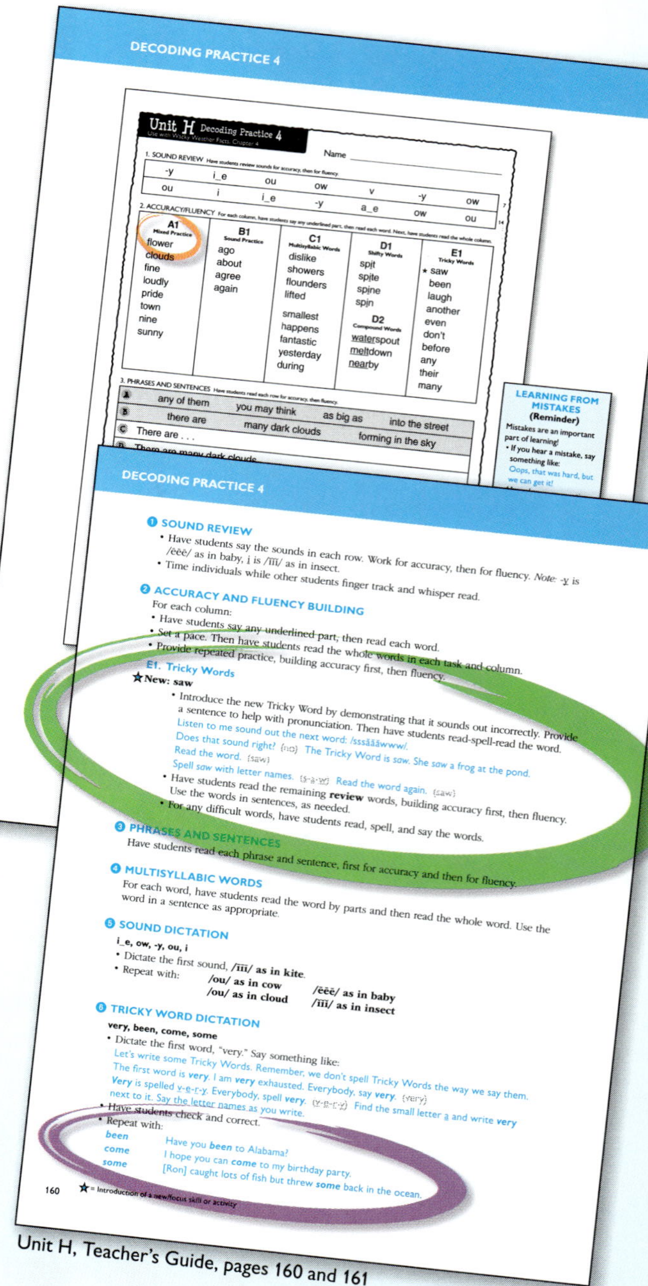

Unit H, Teacher's Guide, pages 160 and 161

Accuracy and Fluency Building

HOW TO PRACTICE SOUNDS IN WORDS

These tasks all follow the same basic steps.

- For each task, have students read any underlined part and then read each word.
  Touch under the first word in C1. Everyone, read the underlined sound and then read the whole word. First word. (/lll/, middle)
  Next word. (/īīī/, sky)
  Next word. (/er/, under)
  Next word. (/ə/, ago)
  Next word. (/ēēē/, three)
  Next word. (/ĭĭĭ/, thin)
  Next word. (/ăăă/, lands)

  Great. Read that a little faster. Start with the first word and keep reading.
  (/lll/, middle; /īīī/, sky; /er/, under; /ə/, ago; /ēēē/, three; /ĭĭĭ/, thin; /er/, under; /ăăă/, lands)

  [Nate], you are doing a nice job of tracking the words with your finger.
  Your turn to read three words.
  (/lll/, middle; /īīī/, sky; /er/, under)
  I'm very proud of you all. You tracked the words and whisper read while [Nate] took his turn. Listen for your turn. [Juanita]. (/lll/, middle)
  [Lisa], next word. (/īīī/, sky) [Jamal] . . .

  Say each sound two times, then say the word. My turn first. Listen. /l/, /l/, middle; /ī/, /ī/, sky; /ə/, /ə/, ago. Your turn.
  Say each sound two times and then the word, but keep going.
  (/l/, /l/, middle; /ī/, /ī/, sky; /er/, /er/, under . . .)

- Have students read the whole words in each task and column.
  Now read the whole words.
  Start with middle. Read with me about this fast
  Set a pace by tapping your desk or modeling.
  Everyone, read the whole words. (middle, sky, under, ago, three, thin, lands)

- Provide repeated practice, building accuracy first, then fluency. Set a slightly faster pace by tapping your desk.

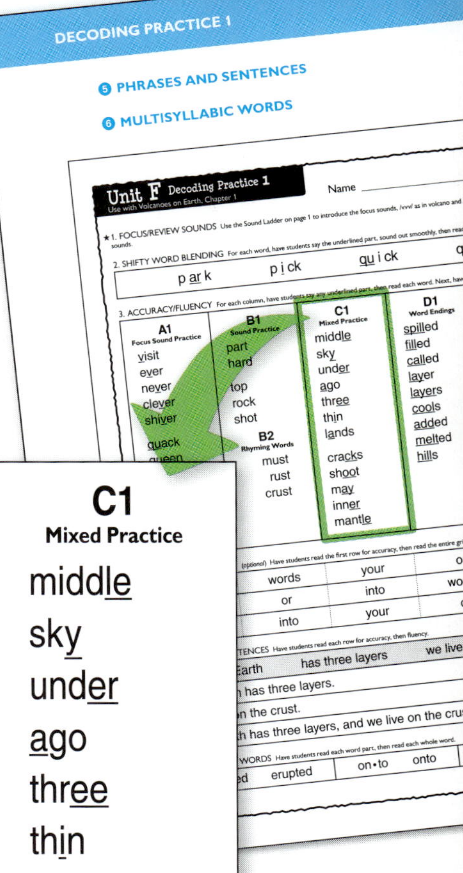

Accuracy and Fluency Building Correction Procedure

SOUNDS IN WORDS: WORKING TOWARD MASTERY, CORRECTING ERRORS

In this example, the student reads "ask" instead of "ash."

[Jose], your turn. (must, ask, trip, crust, blast)

Nice job, [Jose]. There was just one hard word.

Point to the difficult word on the Decoding Practice or write the word on the board or a piece of paper. Point to where the error occurred— the missed sound.

> **TWO SOUNDS**
>
> If a letter has two sounds, tell students which sound to use.

- Provide a group correction to take the attention off the student who made the mistake. Have students correct the missed sound.
  Everyone, what's the last sound in this word? (/shshsh/)

- Have students sound out the word with the correct sound.
  Sound out the word. (/ăăăshshsh/)

- Have students read the word. Then use the word in a sentence.
  Yes, the word is . . . (ash). When the fire burned out, all that was left was . . . ash.

- Practice other words. Return to the difficult word until students read the word correctly on three consecutive attempts.
  Nice job. Everyone, read the whole list.
  (must, ash, trip, crust, blast)

[Juanita], first word. (must)

[Jose], next word. (ash)

Great, you got that hard word.

Everyone, next word. (trip)

Everyone, touch the word *ash*.

Everyone, what's the next word? (trip)

- Give individual turns to the student who missed the word. Acknowledge the student's effort.
  [Jose], what's this word? (ash)

Nod and smile at [Jose].

> **PRACTICE WITH A COLLEAGUE**
>
> **To become proficient at correcting errors:**
>
> 1. Study the script.
> 2. Practice teaching these tasks from any Exercise. Have your colleague make at least one mistake.

> **SUMMARY OF MASTERY-BASED CORRECTIONS**
>
> **Corrected errors are an opportunity to learn.**
>
> - Quickly write any misread word on a chalkboard or piece of paper.
> - Have students correct the missed sound, sound it out, and then say the word. Or use a build-up correction.
> - Use the word in a sentence.
> - Go on to other words. Return to the difficult word until students read the word correctly on three consecutive responses.
> - Acknowledge students' efforts.

Bossy E

Most children know what it means to be bossy, so *Read Well* teaches students that an e on the end of a word is often bossy. The Bossy E tells the vowel to say its name. Arrows on the Accuracy and Fluency Building exercises provide visual support for understanding how the Bossy E works. Initially, words are presented in short-vowel/long-vowel pairs, so students learn how the discrimination works.

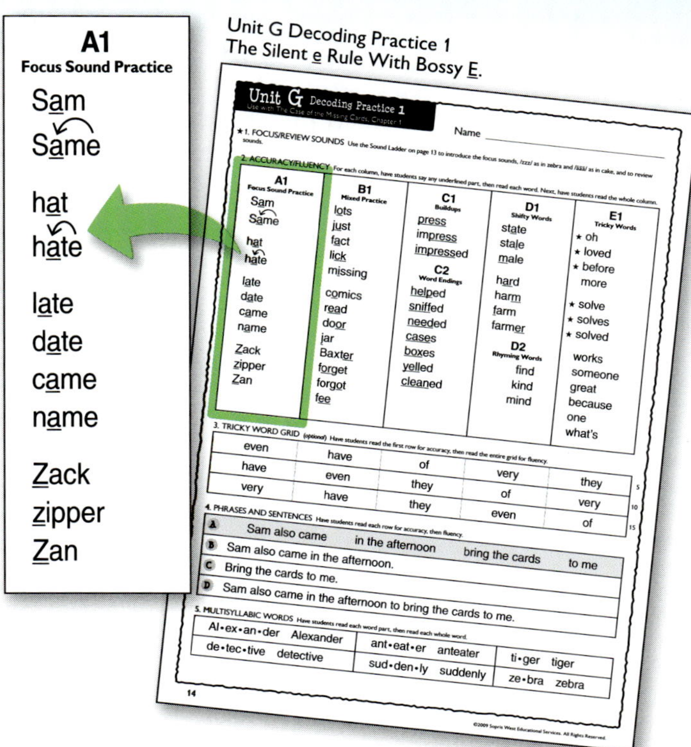

HOW TO TEACH BOSSY E

From Unit G, Decoding Practice 1

- Introduce the short-vowel word. Say something like:
  Look at the first word. Is there an e at the end of this word? (no)
  What is the underlined sound? (/ăăă/)
  Read the word. (Sam)
  Yes, the word is *Sam*. I have a friend named Sam.

- Tell students the letter e at the end of a word is often bossy. Have students look at the next word. Explain that the arrow shows how the Bossy E works. The Bossy E jumps over the m and makes the underlined letter say its name. Say something like:
  Is there an e at the end of the next word? (yes)
  What is the name of the underlined letter? (a)
  Read the word. (same)
  We are all reading the *same* book.
  When we see the Bossy E, we know to say /āāā/.
  The Bossy E makes a say /āāā/ as in *cake*.

- Repeat with "hat" and "hate."

PRACTICE WITH A COLLEAGUE

To learn how to teach the Bossy E:

1. Study the scripted version.

2. Practice with a colleague.

Bossy E

HOW TO TEACH BOSSY E (continued)

- Provide repeated practice, building accuracy first, then fluency.
  Read the whole words again. I'm going to count to three between each word. Touch under the first word. **Pause.**
  First word. (Sam) **Pause.** Next word. (same) **Pause.**
  Next word. (hat) **Pause.** Next word. (hate) **Pause.**
  Next word. (late) **Pause.** Next word. (date) **Pause.**
  Next word. (came) **Pause.** Next word. (name)
  Everyone, touch the word *same.*
  Touch the word *hate.*
  [David], read the next word. (late)

- If your students can easily discriminate long and short vowels, practice Bossy E with abbreviated support. Simply say:
  Read the underlined letter and then the word.
  (/ăăă/, Sam; /āāā/, same; /ăăă/, hat; /āāā/, hate;
  /āāā/, late; /āāā/, date; /āāā/, came; /āāā/, name)

- Complete each task by having students build accuracy and fluency reading the whole words.
  Read the whole words.
  (Sam, same, hat, hate, late, date, came, name)

Bossy E, Correction Procedure

HOW TO CORRECT FOR BOSSY E

In this example, students read "hop" instead of "hope."

Read all of the words. (rode, hop)

- Quickly write any misread word on a chalkboard or piece of paper.
  Oops. Let's look at that second word again.
  Write "hope" on the board.

- Have students correct the sound missed by applying the
  Bossy E rule and then saying the word.
  Is there a Bossy E on the end? (yes)
  So the underlined letter says its name.
  What does it say? (/ōōō/)   Read the word. (hope)

- Use the word in a sentence.
  I *hope* we will read another mystery soon.

- Go on to other words. Return to the difficult word until students
  read the word correctly on three consecutive responses.
  Go back to the top of the list.
  First word. (rode) Next word. (hope)
  Next word. (home)
  Excellent, you got the word *hope.*
  Does *hope* have a Bossy E on the end? (yes)

  So what does the letter o say? (/ōōō/)
  Pick your pencil up and underline the o in *rode, hope, home,*
  and *alone.*
  Put your pencils on the desk above your paper.
  Now read the underlined sound and then the whole word.
  (/ōōō/, rode; /ōōō/, hope; /ōōō/, home; /ōōō/, alone)

  Everyone, touch *hope.* Touch *alone.*

- Give an individual turn to the student who made the error.
  Acknowledge the student's efforts.
  [Jason], your turn. Read the words. (rode, hope, home, alone, these)
  Give me a high five!

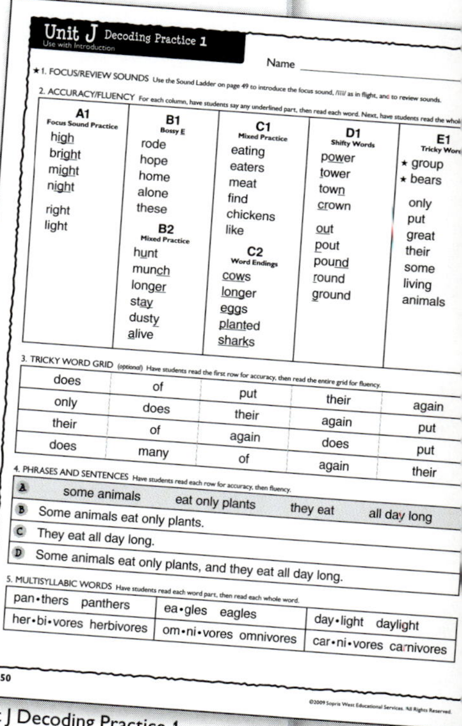

Unit J Decoding Practice 1

Extra Help With the Bossy E Dictation

If students have difficulty using the Bossy E, add dictation exercises to reinforce the
discrimination between CVC words and CVCE words.
Say something like:

You're going to write the word *same.* I have the *same* hat as my friend.
Tell me the word. (same)
Tell me the first sound. (/sss/)   Write it. Next sound. (/ăăă/)   Write it.
Next sound. (/mmm/)   Write it. You've written /săm/.
To make the word say *same,* what does the word need? (Bossy E)
That's right. Put an e on the end. Now read the word. (same)

"

Multisyllabic Words

As students move into more sophisticated text, the number of multisyllabic words increases. To be confident and independent readers, students need to know how to decode and read unknown multisyllabic words with ease and fluency. In *Fluency Foundations* and throughout *Read Well*, students work on recognition of the common letter patterns, or chunks, that sophisticated readers use to fluently decode unknown words.

EXAMPLE

Can you read the following word?

lackmiltoncartwelty

If you were able to read this word, how did you accomplish the task? More than likely, you read the common letter chunks sequentially from left to right—lack•mil•ton•cart•welt•y. This strategy of identifying and reading common letter chunks from left to right builds on skills learned in pattern recognition.

In *Fluency Foundations* and with progressive frequency in *Read Well 2*, students focus on the application of known skills to multisyllabic words. Students will have many opportunities to practice the strategy for figuring out new multisyllabic words.

Multisyllabic Words

Fluency Foundations

On a daily basis in *Fluency Foundations*, students practice reading word patterns (CV, CVC, CVCE, CVVC), words with consonant blends, and words with word endings. Students use their knowledge of systematically reading from left to right and their ability to automatically identify pattern words to read multisyllabic words. Finally, students read the same words in connected text.

For example, in Unit B *Fluency Foundations*, students identify the known word parts in "cricket" and then put them together to read the word. Students loop under and read each word part.

> **Read the first word part.** (crick)
> **Read the next word part.** (et)
> **Say the word.** (cricket)
>
> crick et   cricket

As students move forward, they identify known word parts with abbreviated visual cues. Bullets separate the word parts, and loops are used only to correct errors.

> **Read each part.**
> **First part.** (de)
> **Next part.** (tec)
> **Last part.** (tive)
> **Say the word.** (detective)
>
> de·tec·tive   detective

Multisyllabic Words

HOW TO PRACTICE MULTISYLLABIC WORDS

- For each word, have students read each syllable, then read the whole word. Use the word in a sentence, as appropriate.

  Touch under the first multisyllabic word.
  Read each syllable. (gar-den)
  Read the whole word. (garden)
  My grandmother loves to work in the . . . garden.

  Touch under the next word.
  Read each syllable. (pep-per-mint)
  Read the whole word. (peppermint)
  My grandmother planted . . . peppermint.

  Touch under the next word.
  Read each syllable. (dif-fer-ent)
  Read the whole word. (different)
  I got my haircut. Now I look . . . (different).

  Touch under the next word.
  Read each syllable. (yes-ter-day)
  Read the whole word. (yesterday)
  We went to an assembly . . . (yesterday).

  Touch under the next word.
  Read each syllable. (Ber-tha)
  Read the whole word. (Bertha)
  Do you know anyone named . . . (Bertha)?

  Touch under the next word.
  Read each syllable. (in-ter-est-ing)
  Read the whole word. (interesting)
  I think studying about insects is . . . (interesting).

- Repeat each row to build accuracy and fluency.
  Read each row. (gar-den, garden; pep-per-mint, peppermint; dif-fer-ent, different; yes-ter-day, yesterday; Ber-tha, Bertha; in-ter-est-ing, interesting)

USING SENTENCES

Oral sentences prompt students to use their English oral language skills to pronounce multisyllabic words correctly.

EXERCISE 4

1 SOUND REVIEW
Have students read the sounds and key word phrases. Work for accuracy, then fluency.
Read the sounds and the phrases. (/oo/ as in blue, /ir/ as in bird, /aw/ as in paw, /ai/ as in rain)

2 SHIFTY WORD BLENDING
For each word, have students say the underlined sound. Then have them sound out the word smoothly and say it. Use the words in sentences, as appropriate.

3 ACCURACY AND FLUENCY BUILDING
- For each task, have students say any underlined part, then read the word.
- Set a pace. Then have students read the whole words in each task and column.
- Provide repeated practice, building accuracy first, then fluency, independent of your voice.

E1. Tricky Words
For each Tricky Word, have students identify known sounds or word parts. Use the word in a sentence to help with pronunciation.

hours	Our school day is about six . . . hours.
love	The family got a new puppy. They all . . . love . . . the puppy.
early	I don't like to be late, so I get up . . . early.
friendly	Minnie Bird is very . . . friendly.
only	There was just one apple left. There was . . . only one.
laughed	The puppy was funny. We all . . . laughed.

E2. Story Words
Tell students the underlined sound, then have them read the word.

4 READING BY ANALOGY
Have students figure out how to say o- by reading other words they know.

5 MULTISYLLABIC WORDS
For each word, have students read each syllable and then read the whole word. Use the word in a sentence, as appropriate.

evening	It gets dark outside in the . . . evening.
peppers	Emma ate some chili with hot . . . peppers.
habitat	For many animals, the rain forest is their . . . habitat.
postcard	My friend sent me a . . . postcard.
suddenly	The firecracker went off . . . suddenly.
hesitated	I was afraid to jump into the cold water, so I . . . hesitated.

6 WORDS IN CONTEXT
- Tell students to use the sounds and word parts they know and then the sentence to figure out how to say each word. Assist, as needed.
- Have students read each word part, the whole word, and then the sentence.
  Look at the first word in Row A. Thumbs up when you know the word.
  Now read the sentence. (Miss Tim went to Africa to see the wildlife.)
  Everyone, what's the underlined word? (wildlife.)

5 MULTISYLLABIC WORDS
For each word, have students read each syllable and then read the whole word. Use the word in a sentence, as appropriate.

evening	It gets dark outside in the . . . *evening.*
peppers	Emma ate some chili with hot . . . *peppers.*
habitat	For many animals, the rain forest is their . . . *habitat.*
postcard	My friend sent me a . . . *postcard.*
suddenly	The firecracker went off . . . *suddenly.*
hesitated	I was afraid to jump into the cold water, so I . . . *hesitated.*

Tricky Words

Purpose

Tricky Words are irregular. They do not conform to the most common sound-spellings of English and are sometimes not readily decoded by sounding out.

Tricky Words may also include story words for which students have not yet been taught the sounds. These words become decodable once those sounds are taught.

Teaching To Mastery

Tricky Words are introduced gradually. If you teach to mastery in each unit, the Tricky Words stay manageable for students. *Fluency Foundations* and *Read Well 2* introduces Tricky Words before they appear in stories, and they provide multiple opportunities for students to practice reading and writing the words.

REMINDER

Do not teach high-frequency word lists on the side. *Read Well* teaches high-frequency words (both decodable and irregular) in a systematic, decodable sequence.

By the end of *Fluency Foundations*, students will have mastered 99 of the first 100 words from Fry's Word List.

By *Read Well 2* Unit 12, students will master 199 of the top 200 words from Fry's Word List. They will have learned 298 of the top 300 words and 394 of the top 400 words from Fry's Word List.

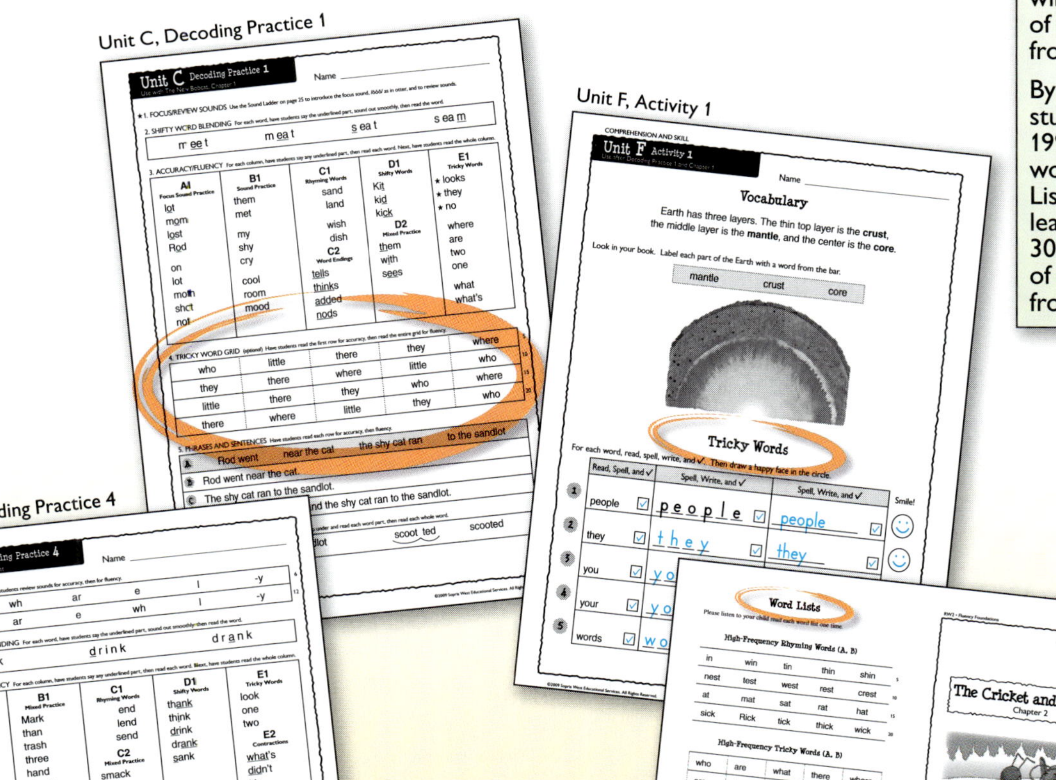

Unit C, Decoding Practice 1

Unit F, Activity 1

Unit B, Decoding Practice 4

Unit B, Homework 2

Tricky Words

HOW TO TEACH TRICKY WORDS IN *FLUENCY FOUNDATIONS*

When introducing irregular words, point out what is regular and what is *tricky* by focusing student attention on all of the letters in the word.

Reading Tricky Words in Fluency Foundations

Follow this procedure for introducing Tricky Words in Decoding Practice. Suggestions for teaching specific Tricky Words are found in each *Fluency Foundations* teacher's guide.

- For most words, tell students the Tricky Word. Then point out familiar sounds.
  This word is what. Say the word. (what)

- Demonstrate how the word is mispronounced when sounded out. Then guide students to say it correctly.
  If we sounded it out, it would sound like this: /whăăăt/.
  Do we say, "/Whăăăt/ are you doing?"
  No, that's silly.
  We say . . . what. Read the word. (what)

- Have students spell the word with letter names and read it again.
  Spell what with letter names. (w-h-a-t)
  Read the word again. (what)

As students build a bank of Tricky Words, they use words they know to read rhyming words (e.g., do, to, into). They also use known words as buildups for new words (e.g., was, wasn't, would, wouldn't).

Writing Tricky Words in *Fluency Foundations*

By writing Tricky Words, children learn the words through a combination of pattern knowledge and memorization. Students write words in *Fluency Foundations* Decoding Practice 4 and in independent work.

Basic instructions: For each word, have students read or say it, then orally spell and write it. Demonstrate and have students cross out the entire word and rewrite the entire word, as needed.

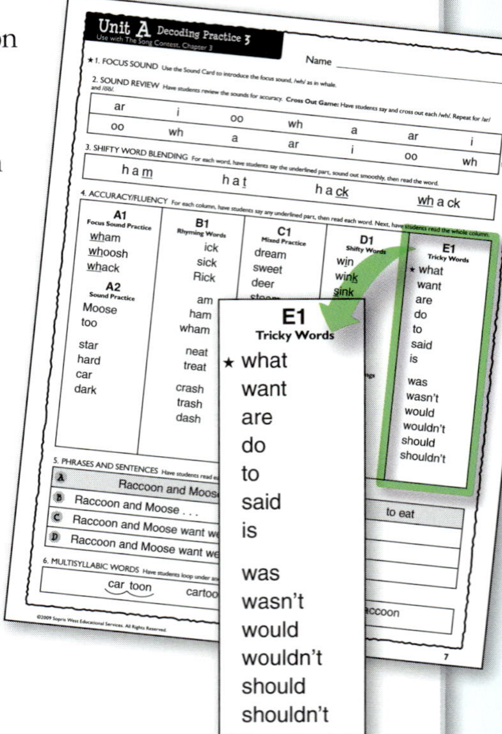

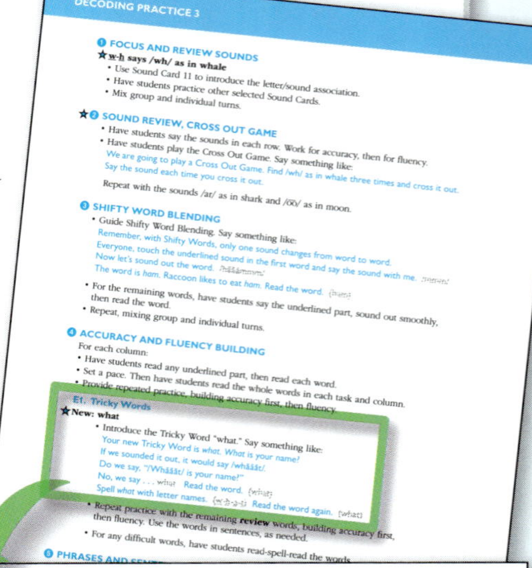

Unit A Teacher's Guide, page 34

Tricky Words, Correction Procedures

HOW TO CORRECT A TRICKY WORD ERROR

Study the script for how to correct a Tricky Word error.

Everyone, read the Tricky Words. (many, another, water, Earth, again, were, where, give)

Excellent, go back to the top.

[Natalie, your turn]. (many)

[Andy]. (another)

[Everyone, two words]. (water, Earth)

[Loran]. (again)

[Wren]. (where)

In this example, student says "where" instead of "were." Write the words "were" and "where" on the board.

[Wren], that's a very tricky word.
Let's work on it a bit. It will help all of us.

Point to "were." Everyone, look at the word and spell it. (w-e-r-e)

That's the word *were*. We *were* happy to improve our reading fluency.

Say the word. (were) Now spell it. (w-e-r-e)

What's the word? (were)

[Wren], use the word *were* in a sentence. We . . . (were happy).

Point to "where." Now look at the next word. It looks a lot like the word *were*, but it isn't. What's different? (It's longer. It has an h.)

That's exactly right. That's the word *where*.

Where are we?

Say the word. (where) Now spell it with a loud h. (w-H-e-r-e)

Everyone, read the whole list. (many, another, water, Earth, again, were, where, give)

[Everyone], touch *Earth*. Now read the rest of the list.

(Earth, again, were, where, give)

[Natalie], touch the word *water*.

Wren, touch the word *were*.

Everyone, read the last two words. (where, give)

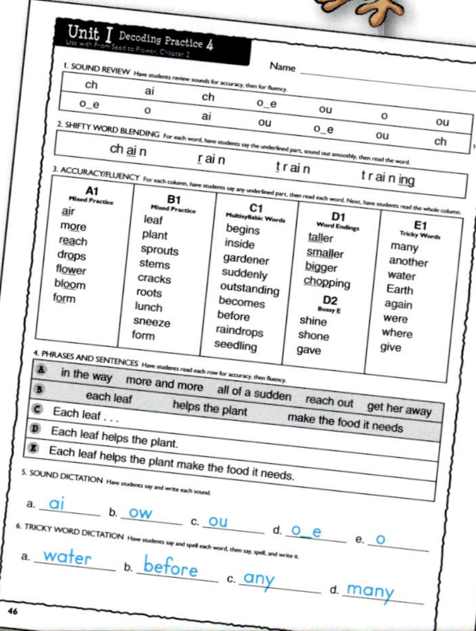

Decoding Practice Summary

TEACH WELL

Diagnostic teaching becomes natural with practice. Correct gently and celebrate learning.

ENJOY

Smile.

Smile.

Smile.

TEACH WELL

- Provide gentle group corrections.
- Provide diagnostic corrections.
- Then practice to mastery.

HAVE FUN

Use little voices.
Use **BIG** voices.
Use grumpy voices.
Use *chirpy* voices.
Use squeaky voices.
Use **STRONG** voices.

BE WOWFUL!

Wow! [Justin] was able to read that **BIG** word without my help.

How did you do that, [Justin]?

SUMMARY OF MASTERY-BASED CORRECTIONS

- Quickly write any misread word on a chalkboard or piece of paper. Have students correct the missed sound, sound it out, and then say the word. Or use a build-up correction.

- Use the word in a sentence.

- Go on to other words. Return to the difficult word until students read the word correctly on three consecutive responses.

- Acknowledge students' efforts.

How to Teach Introductions and Story Reading

In this section:

Preparing to Teach Story Reading

After daily Daily Decoding, students engage in Story Reading.

Previewing Instruction

Each day, students complete a balanced daily lesson. This section will help you learn Story Reading, the components of Teacher-Directed Lesson Part 2. Preview the Story Reading directions in the unit teacher's guide before teaching your small group. When teaching, simply follow the numbered tasks.

Preparing to Teach Story Reading

In *Fluency Foundations*, Story Reading is teacher-directed oral story reading. During these sessions, teachers monitor students' abilities to apply decoding skills accurately, expressively, and fluently in connected text. Comprehension building occurs as teachers prompt lively interactive discussions while students read.

Each *Fluency Foundations* Decoding Practice is followed by a teacher-directed Story Reading.

Students read a new story each day.

Through Story Reading, students:

- become accurate, expressive, and fluent readers.
- develop English oral language through discussions.
- develop literal and inferential comprehension skills.
- learn to monitor comprehension.
- build vocabulary knowledge.
- build content knowledge.
- learn to summarize expository information and retell narrative stories.

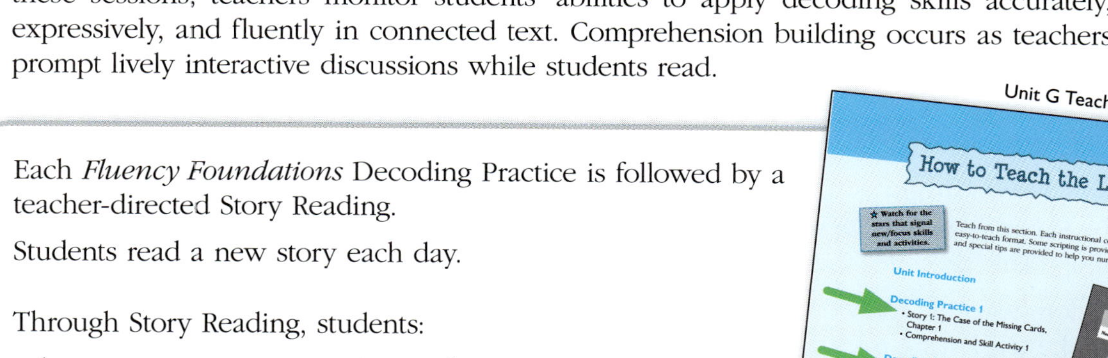

Unit G Teacher's Guide, page 75

4-DAY PLAN • *Fluency Core*

Day 1	Day 2	Day 3	Day 4
• Unit Introduction • Decoding Practice 1 • Story 1: The Case of the Missing Cards, Ch. 1 • Comprehension and Skill Activity 1 • Homework 1	• Decoding Practice 2 • Story 2: The Case of the Missing Cards, Ch. 2 • Comprehension and Skill Activities 2, 3 • Homework 2	• Decoding Practice 3 • Story 3: The Case of the Missing Cards, Ch. 3 • Comprehension and Skill Activities 4, 5 • Homework 3	• Decoding Practice 4 • Story 4: The Case of the Missing Cards, Ch. 4 • Comprehension and

6-DAY PLAN • *Intervention*

Day 1	Day 2	Day 3	Day 4
• Unit Introduction • Decoding Practice 1 • Story 1: The Case of the Missing Cards, Ch. 1 • Comprehension and Skill Activity 1 • Homework 1	• Decoding Practice 2 • Story 2: The Case of the Missing Cards, Ch. 2 • Comprehension and Skill Activities 2, 3 • Homework 2	• Decoding Practice 3 • Story 3: The Case of the Missing Cards, Ch. 3 • Comprehension and Skill Activities 4, 5 • Homework 3	• Decoding Practice 4 • Story 4: The Case of the Missing Cards, Ch. 4 • Comprehension and Skill Activities 6, 7 • Homework 4
Day 5 Extra Practice 1 • Decoding • Fluency Passage • Activity • Homework: Fluency Passage	**Day 6** Extra Practice 2 • Decoding • Fluency Passage • Activity • Homework: Fluency Passage		

Unit Introductions

In *Fluency Foundations*, each unit includes an introduction. These openers are tailored to the genre and story content. Students learn to apply their prior knowledge, make predictions, identify genres, and review or learn new vocabulary.

Narrative Example: Unit G, *The Case of the Missing Cards*

In *Fluency Foundations*, the unit introduction is presented with the first page of the unit. (This precedes the day's Decoding Practice and Story Reading.)

Before teaching, preview the sample script in the teacher's guides. Scripting provides you with a model for how to prompt connections with prior knowledge, make predictions, and introduce or review vocabulary and content knowledge.

In Unit G, students read a mystery—a genre first introduced in *Read Well 1*.

❶ Title/Topic
Students preview a new book or story, identifying the title/topic.

❷ Deepening Vocabulary
Vocabulary is introduced with a student-friendly explanation. Then, students immediately use the words.

❸ Predictions
Students make predictions based on their prior knowledge; students predict what will happen.

❹ Genre (Text Structure)
In Unit G, students relearn what a mystery is.

1. Introducing the Topic

**Viewing; Identifying—Main Characters, Genre; Building Knowledge;
Defining and Using Vocabulary—detective, mystery; Predicting; Inferring**
Have students identify the characters and genre for Unit G.
Let's take a look at the picture on the Introduction.
The zebra and the anteater are the main characters in this unit.
Touch the zebra. His name is Zack.
Touch the anteater. His name is Alexander.
Zack and Alexander are detectives.
A *detective* is someone who looks for things and solves problems.
What do you think Zack and Alexander will do in this story?

This story is called a *mystery*. What kind of story is it? (a mystery)
In a mystery, there is a problem that needs to be solved, or there is something strange going on that needs to be explained.

Who do you think will solve the mystery?
(The detectives will solve the mystery.)

Unit Introductions

Expository Example: Unit F—*VOLCANOES ON EARTH*

In Unit F, students read four expository passages about volcanoes.

❶ Topic

Students identify the topic by discussing the picture or text.

❷ Genre

Students identify whether they think the story will have factual content or be make-believe.

❸ Priming Background Knowledge

Students brainstorm what they already know about volcanoes.

The following two panels show the Unit Introduction teacher material, first in a smaller reproduction and then enlarged:

1. Introducing the Topic

Viewing; Identifying—Topic; Priming Background Knowledge; Defining and Using Vocabulary—volcano, erupt; Building Knowledge
Have students identify the topic of Unit F.

Let's take a look at the picture on the Introduction.
Look at the picture. What do you see? (a volcano)
How can you tell it is a volcano?

Yes, a *volcano* is a mountain that has erupted or can still erupt.
Who can tell me what *erupt* means? (shoot out, blow steam . . .)
That's right. *Erupt* means shoot out. When a volcano erupts, it shoots out lava, rock, and ash.

In this unit, you're going to learn scientific terms that explain how volcanoes are formed and what happens when they erupt.
You're also going to read two factual passages about volcanoes that erupted.
One volcano erupted in Pompeii almost 2000 years ago. The other erupted in the state of Washington in 1980. That volcano is still active. Sometimes, people can see steam rising from the volcano's crater.

What do you already know about volcanoes?

Watch for information you already know and information that adds to your knowledge.

Story Reading

Research Snapshot

Guided Repeated Oral Reading
The National Reading Panel (2000) concluded that "guided oral reading procedures that included guidance from teachers, peers, or parents had a significant and positive impact on word recognition, fluency, and comprehension across a range of grade levels" (p. 12).

Story Reading With the Teacher • First Reading

Each Story Reading in *Fluency Foundations* follows the same general procedures.

UNPRACTICED READING

The first reading allows you to monitor how well students read and comprehend new passages.

ACTIVE STUDENT ENGAGEMENT

Mix group and individual turns to keep all students actively engaged.

Have students track text with their fingers. Tracking text during group work helps students read accurately, ensures that students pay attention, and reduces interruptions caused by lost places.

ACCURACY

Accurate reading is a prerequisite to good comprehension. During Story Reading, gently correct errors. Have the student reread the sentence. Count and record errors.

After Story Reading, put difficult words on the board and practice with the group.

Note: Read Well students read well. Accuracy goals are set at independent levels. Reread the story if accuracy goals are not met on the first reading.

Unit J Teacher's Guide, page 272

First Reading • Comprehension

COMPREHENDING AS YOU GO

Keep the focus of Story Reading on comprehension. Ask gray-text questions when indicated. Prompts direct students' attention to:

- information central to understanding the story

- information needed to make inferences and draw conclusions

Prompts also encourage students to use vocabulary in context.

MONITORING COMPREHENSION AND FIX-UP STRATEGIES

Gray-text questions allow you to monitor comprehension throughout Story Reading.

- Share your thinking as you discuss text.

- When comprehension breaks down, teach students how to use fix-up strategies. (See page 82.)

ENGLISH ORAL LANGUAGE

Teach and encourage students to respond in complete sentences. Restate answers. Say something like:

What's the chapter title?
(I Wish I May, I Wish I Might)
That's right. The chapter title is . . .
"I Wish I May, I Wish I Might."

As appropriate, have students repeat the complete sentence.

Irma the Discontented Cow, Storybook Unit J

IRMA THE DISCONTENTED COW

Chapter 1
I Wish I May, I Wish I Might

Irma the cow was an herbivore. To get enough food, she had to eat grass all day, day after day. Irma was a discontented herbivore.

What do you know about Irma?

Irma stood in deep green grass. She	7
grumbled, "Graze, graze, graze! That is all I do	16
all day long. I hate being an animal that eats	26
only plants." Irma was discontented. That	32
means that she was not happy with her life.	41

"Stop complaining," said the other cows.	47
"We are lucky to be cows. We do not need to	58
hunt for food. We graze all day on grass and	68
weeds."	69

How does Irma feel? Why is Irma *discontented*?

50

Answering in complete sentences serves as a scaffold to written responses.

How does Irma feel? Why is Irma *discontented*?

NOTES FROM OUR FEATHERED FRIENDS

Watch for the sign holders in the teacher's guides. Notes are provided to help you periodically focus on vocabulary, comprehension, and prosody.

◆◆ = Critical for ELLs and children with language delays, but recommended for all students.

Story Reading With the Teacher

First Reading • Accuracy

Omissions, insertions, and misread words all disrupt and/or alter comprehension of text. Starting with Unit A of *Fluency Foundations,* students learn to read accurately.

HOW TO TEACH STUDENTS TO READ WITH ACCURACY

Write a sentence from the day's story on the board. Then have students catch your errors. Have fun.

Moose ran to the trees.

Say something like:

Our job is to learn to read accurately. It is important to read the words the author wrote.

Listen to me read the sentence on the board. If you hear a mistake, raise your finger.

Raise your index finger. Show me what you will do if you hear a mistake.

Point to each word as you read.
Listen to me read. "Moose ran *on* the trees." [Marisa], you caught a mistake. What did you hear?
(It says *to.*)

Great, [Marisa]. I read *on* instead of *to.* Moose didn't run *on* the trees.
Everyone, read the sentence. (Moose ran to the trees.)

Focus During Story Reading

- Keep the focus on comprehension.

- Acknowledge accurate reading.
  When students read, say things like:
  [Juan], that was great. You read carefully.

- Gently correct errors.
  If a student makes an error during Story Reading, model and have the student reread. If the student reads: Moose said/was near the stream . . .
  Say something like: Yes, it says Moose was near . . .
  Read that one more time. (Moose was near the stream . . .)
  Excellent! That sounded very smooth.

Unit A, *The Song Contest*

Chapter 1
The Big Event

It was time for the big Song Contest. The first contestant was Moose. This big mammal represented the herbivores, or plant-eating animals. It was time to begin.

Deer said, "Moose!" 3

Moose was near the stream with weeds in 11
his teeth. Swoosh! Moose ran to the trees. "I 20
can do this," he said. "Oo, oo! I am a moose." 31

What is the big event? What kind of animal is Moose?

6

First Reading • Decoding Strategies in Context

As students progress through *Fluency Foundations*, continue monitoring accurate reading, but also encourage students to quickly use their decoding strategies when they encounter difficult words.

HOW TO TEACH STUDENTS TO APPLY STRATEGIES

Write a sentence from the day's story on the board. Demonstrate and guide.

Wiggy is the <u>reporter</u> of wacky weather facts for RWF-TV.

Say something like:
Sometimes, we will run into hard words. Good readers don't worry. They just keep reading by sounding out and reading the word by parts.
Watch and listen to me.

Let's pretend the hard word is the underlined word. I'm a good reader, so I'm going to start sounding it out by parts. I'm going to go for it. Listen. "Wiggy is the rrreee-port-er reporter of wacky weather facts."

What did I do with the hard word?
(You sounded it out and read it by parts.)
Right. If you run into a hard word, what should you do?
(Sound it out and read it by parts.)

Focus During Story Reading

- Keep the focus of Story Reading on comprehension.

- If a student stalls, quickly guide sounding out and reading the word by parts.
  If a student reads: (Meet Wiggy . . .)
  Begin sounding out with the student: /Wwwēēēsel/.
  Right. What does it say? (Meet Wiggy Weasel.)
  Excellent. I liked the way you jumped in and helped sound out *weasel.*

- Quickly redirect students to the meaning of the story.
  Everyone, point to Wiggy Weasel in the picture.
  What is a weasel? (an animal)
  Everyone, read the first paragraph together. (Meet Wiggy Weasel. Wiggy is the reporter of wacky weather facts for RWF-TV.)

Story Reading With the Teacher

First Reading • Monitoring Comprehension and Fix-up Strategies

As students progress through *Fluency Foundations*, continually teach students to monitor and fix up comprehension.

LITERAL COMPREHENSION

Gray-text questions will help you keep the focus of Story Reading on comprehension. Questions direct students to review, rehearse, use, and summarize important information. Literal comprehension provides the framework for making references.

- Share your thinking. Say something like:
  The question is: What did Harriet and her friends sing? I remember that they sang, but I don't remember what they sang.

- Initially, tell students how to fix up comprehension by looking back and rereading. When students know what to do, have them state the strategy.
  What can we do? (Look back and reread.)

  That's right. When did Harriet and her friends sing? At the beginning, middle, or end of this chapter? (end)

  Look at the end of the story. Find what Harriet and her friends sang. Put your finger under the first words of the song.

- Have students reread.
  Everyone, reread the first sentence.
  (Free at last! Free at last!)

- Restate the question
  That's right. What did Harriet sing?
  (Free at last! Free at last!)

- Have students continue reading, as appropriate.
  Look at the picture on the next page. What is Harriet doing?
  (leading people to freedom)
  That's right, and what did they sing when they got there? (free at last)

- If responses are verbatim, paraphrase or have students paraphrase, when appropriate.

HARRIET TUBMAN ESCAPES

Chapter 2
Follow That Star

Who is the story about? What did Harriet want? What would she need to do to get what she wanted?

Harriet Tubman was a slave, but she wanted to be free. One night, Harriet ran away from her owner. Her father told her to follow the North Star. He told her to follow the moss that grows on the north side of the trees.

Harriet looked for the star. She ran far	8
to be free. She looked for the moss on the	18
trees. She ran farther and farther.	24
Harriet ran until she was free! At last, she	33
could do what she wanted.	38
After Harriet was free, she worked hard to	46
free her friends. Harriet took her friends from	54
farm to farm. She hid them in the dark. They	64
ran to be free.	68
Harriet and her friends sang, "Free at last!	76
Free at last!"	79

How did Harriet get her freedom? How did Harriet help others? What did Harriet and her friends sing?

38

How did Harriet get her freedom? How did Harriet help others? What did Harriet and her friends sing?

Unit D, *Harriet Tubman Escapes.* page 38

Story Reading With the Teacher

As students progress through Fluency Foundations, continually, teach students to monitor and fix up comprehension.

INFERENTIAL COMPREHENSION

Story introductions, note boxes from our feathered friends, and gray text questions periodically model how to help students with inferential questions.

If comprehension fails, tailor your discussion to the question.

- Have students identify whether the information is in the book or needs to be figured out.

- Have students reread, as appropriate, looking for clues.

- Help students make connections with what they know.

- Provide additional background knowledge, if needed.

- Think aloud. Share your thinking. Have students share their thinking. Think together.

This example demonstrates how to guide inferential thinking. The last question in this chapter asks, "Why is Harriet Tubman an important person in history?"

- Identify whether the book tells the answer.
  The book tells us what Harriet Tubman did. It's up to us to figure out from clues in the book why she is so important that she is remembered today.

- Think together.
  Let's think together. We need to figure out what Harriet Tubman did that made her special. What made her special? (She was a slave.)
  Yes, she was a slave. What did she do to become free? (She ran away.)
  Yes, Harriet ran to freedom. Is that the end of her story? (no)
  What else did she do? (She helped other people.)
  That's right. Listen to me read the last part of the chapter again. "Harriet Tubman was brave. She worked hard for what she believed was right. She helped more than *300 people* escape to freedom." How many people did Harriet help? (more than 300 people)

- Restate the question and have students explain their thinking using what they know.
  Why is Harriet Tubman an important person in history? She ran to freedom and then . . .
  she helped more than 300 other people escape.

- Clarify or explain how you figured out the answer.
  That's right. She helped hundreds of people escape to freedom.
  We figured out why Harriet Tubman was an important person in history.
  We did that by thinking about what we learned in the story.

SECOND READING

Second readings alternate Short Passage Practice with Timed Readings. In Short Passage Practice, students work on prosody—expression, phrasing, and voice (see Repeated Readings, Section 5.4).

Repeated Readings

Research Snapshot

Repeated Readings, Validated by Research

Dowhower (1987), in a study with second grade students who had average or better decoding ability but below-average reading rate, found that accuracy, comprehension, and prosodic reading (reading in meaningful phrases) were all significantly improved by repeated reading. Dowhower also found that "gains in repeated reading of practiced passages transferred to unpracticed, similar passages" (p. 389).

The more a child reads, the stronger a reader he or she becomes. As students master basic reading processes, they are well on their way to reading almost anything they might choose.

After the first reading, students reread the selection or portions of the selection with the teacher. Rereading with the teacher includes procedures to build prosody and fluency.

The second reading is either:

- Short Passage Practice, or
- Timed Readings

Students also engage daily in:

- Partner Reading (done during daily independent work)
- Homework

Improving Prosody—Expression, Phrasing, and Fluency

In *Fluency Foundations*, many of the Story Readings include Short Passage Practice. Short Passage Practice provides explicit instruction in prosody—expression, phrasing, and fluency.

- Tell students how to read a short passage—a paragraph or two, depending on length.
  Say something like:
  I'm going to read the first two paragraphs. In the second sentence, there's a great action word—zipped. I'm going to emphasize it, or make it stand out with my voice, because it tells us how the detectives went into the room.

- Demonstrate how to read the short passage at a rate slightly faster than the student's rate. Exaggerate expression.
  Zack and Alexander were trying to solve the case of the missing ABC cards. When they got to the school, pause they zipped into Miss Zan's room.

- Guide students as they read the same short passage. Lead with your voice.
  Read those sentences with me.
  Zack and Alexander . . .

- Have the student read the passage independently. Do not read with students.
  [Georgiana], your turn.
  (Zack and Alexander . . .)

- Provide descriptive feedback.
  That was a wonderful reading. It was smooth, and you emphasized the action word zipped.

PRACTICE WITH A COLLEAGUE

1. Read the directions for Short Passage Practice.

2. Using the passage, demonstrate reading at a rate slightly faster than the student's rate. Read smoothly and expressively.

3. Have your colleague read with you.

4. Have your colleague read alone.

5. Provide descriptive feedback.

THE CASE OF THE MISSING CARDS

Chapter 3
The First Clue

What do you think this chapter will be about?

Zack and Alexander were trying to solve the case of the missing ABC cards.   14

When they got to the school, they zipped to Miss Zan's room.   26

"The detectives are here," said Tom. He was impressed with their fast work.   39

Miss Zan said, "My, my! I lost my cards!"   48

Where does this chapter take place? Why is Miss Zan upset? What will Zack and Alexander try to do? Why was Tom impressed with the

Timed Readings

In *Fluency Foundations*, many Story Readings include timed readings.

Timed Reading Procedures:

- Have individual students read the story while the other children track the text with their fingers and whisper read.

- Time individuals for 30 seconds and encourage each student to work for his or her personal best.

- Count the number of words read correctly in 30 seconds (words read minus errors). Multiply by two to determine words read correctly per minute. Record student scores.

THE CASE OF THE MISSING CARDS

Chapter 4
Case Solved!

What do you think will happen in this chapter? Do you think the *detectives* will find Baxter? Will they find the cards?

The detectives were hot on the trail of Baxter Bat. They were trying to find Miss Zan's ABC cards. Zack, Alexander, Tom, and Miss Zan jumped in the jeep and zoomed along the streets. They needed to go to Baxter Bat's cave.   8 · 16 · 22 · 30 · 37 · 42

When they got to the woods, they jumped off the jeep and zigzagged past the trees on foot.   50 · 59 · 60

Soon they were at Baxter's cave. "Baxter, Baxter," they called.   67 · 70

"What is it?" asked a sleepy Baxter. "What is the problem?"   77 · 81

"The ABC cards are missing from Miss Zan's room!" said Tom.   88 · 92

"I have the cards," said Baxter.   98

Who did the detectives find? Where did they find Baxter?

22

THE CASE OF THE MISSING CARDS

"What are you doing with the cards?" asked Miss Zan.   7 · 10

"I was helping a beaver say the letter names. Didn't you tell me to work with a beaver?" asked Baxter.   18 · 27 · 30

"No," said Miss Zan. "I said that you work like an eager beaver! That means you work hard!"   38 · 46 · 48

"Oh!" said Baxter. "I misunderstood!"   53

"Case solved!" said Zack.   57

Who had the missing cards? Why did Baxter take the cards?

23

Partner Reading

Partner reading provides students with multiple opportunities to improve their fluency. Partner reading should be a part of daily independent work once students have learned to manage the activity. Partner Reading begins in Unit A. Partner Reading provides important practice and also teaches students to work productively with another student.

Guide and monitor practice until students demonstrate their ability to do Partner Reading efficiently and responsibly.

PROCEDURES FOR PARTNER READING

1. Pair each student with another student who reads at about the same rate.

2. Teach students how to do Partner Reading.

   - Have two students demonstrate Partner Reading. Say something like:
     Today, you get to learn how to do Partner Reading. [Mike] and [Daeshawna] are going to show us how. [Mike] and [Daeshawna], please bring your books and sit next to each other.

   - Show the students how to sit next to each other so that they face in opposite directions. They can sit on the floor or at desks. Have students open their books and lay them flat. Say something like:
     [Daeshawna] is going to track each word [Mike] reads.
     She is going to do Finger Tracking.
     [Daeshawna], do Finger Tracking while [Mike] reads.
     Everyone, watch [Daeshawna] and [Mike].
     Did [Daeshawna] follow every word [Mike] read? (yes)
     Nice job, [Daeshawna]. By tracking, you are getting practice too.
     Now it will be [Daeshawna's] turn to read.
     What do you think [Mike] is going to do? (Finger Tracking)

   - Have student pairs sit at designated *partner stations*. Assign seats and/or mark locations with tape or signs.

   - Monitor and provide positive feedback as children practice.

   - Teach students to give positive feedback to their partners. Say something like:
     As the listener, you should compliment the reader.
     You could say, "You read with great expression," or "You read very carefully."

     After you have given the reader a compliment, you can say something like:
     "I think I heard just one mistake. Nice job."

     If you are the reader, you should thank your listener. Say something like: "Thank you for listening carefully to me."

   - Guide daily Partner Reading until students are successful without supervision. Then assign Partner Reading as part of independent work.

How to Practice

Practice teaching any Story Reading with a colleague or group of colleagues. When teaching children, you will be multitasking; therefore, it is important to practice beforehand. Have your colleague make one or two decoding errors and one error in comprehension.

HOW TO PRACTICE STORY READING

- Following the teacher's guide, introduce the story and story vocabulary, as indicated.

- During the reading, prompt group and individual turns. Record and gently correct errors. After the reading, practice any difficult words.

- Ask questions as indicated by the gray text in the student storybook. If students have difficulty with a comprehension question, think aloud with them or reread the portion of the story that answers the question.

Practice teaching a Story Reading a second time. This time, do all the things listed above, but also incorporate the next procedures:

- Quickly and unobtrusively, praise students for tracking text with their fingers. (This increases attention and practice by all students.)

- Encourage expressive reading.

- Follow the directions in any note from our feathered friends in the teacher's guide.

GENERAL TIPS

1. Work first on accuracy. Work next on accuracy and expression. Finally, work on accuracy, expression, and fluency.

2. Watch for any ★ that indicates a change in the basic procedure.

3. In general, students should repeat readings as many times as possible.

4. Be sure to have students track text with their fingers.

5. Monitor and build comprehension.

Comprehension and Skill Work

Each day, small groups complete a balanced daily lesson. This section will help you learn to teach the individual tasks involved in Comprehension and Skill Work.

In this section:

6.1 Overview

6.2 Explicit Instruction

Overview • Comprehension and Skill Work

Skill Work

Fluency Foundations includes activities that are used to teach students to work independently while strengthening phonemic awareness, letter/sound associations, recognition of rhyming words, and their ability to write legibly.

TRICKY WORDS
Students practice reading, spelling, and writing high-frequency Tricky Words.

HANDWRITING FLUENCY
Handwriting fluency is critical for success with written responses and composition.

RHYMING PATTERNS
Students work on spelling and recognition of word patterns.

READING FLUENCY
This activity provides additional reading fluency practice.

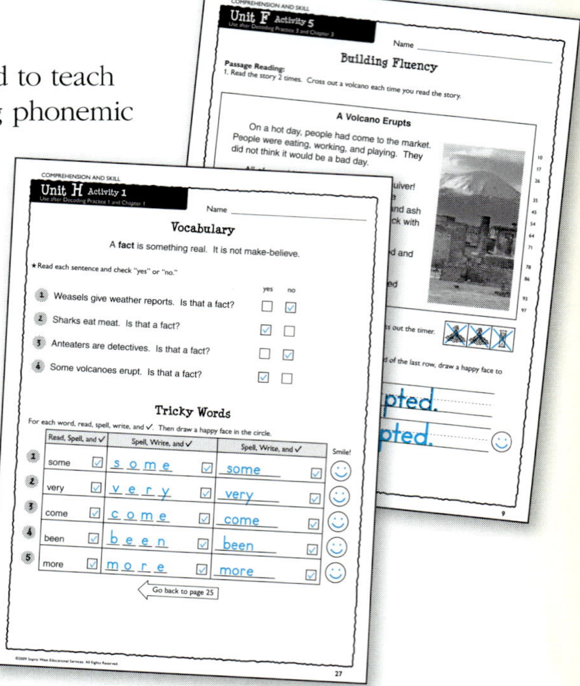

Comprehension Work

Fluency Foundations activities require selection responses that include multiple choice, sentence completion, and sentence writing.

STORY/PASSAGE COMPREHENSION
Remember, Understand, Apply
The Story and Passage Comprehension Activities include items that require students to identify important story elements, illustrate, locate information, make judgments, describe, classify, and predict.

VOCABULARY
Students practice defining and using vocabulary.

STORY MAP/WRITTEN DETAIL
Students retell the stories they've read using guided formats to prepare students for full written retells.

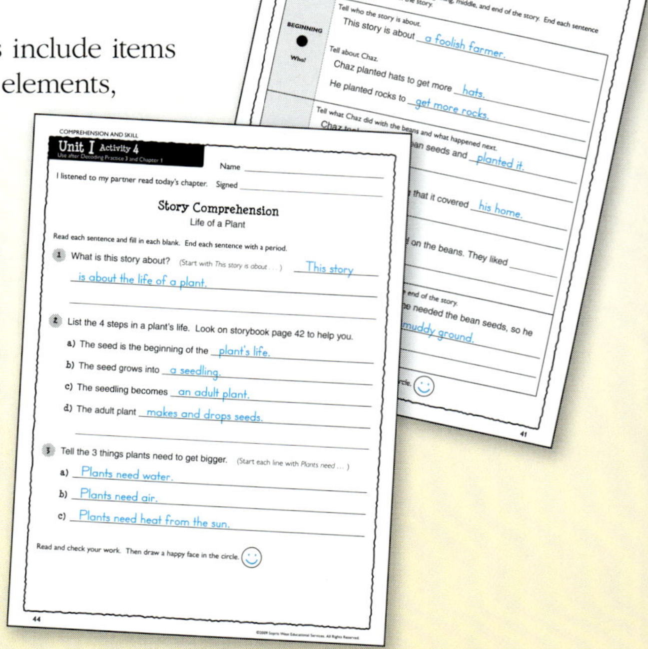

Expectations for Written Work

HIGH EXPECTATIONS

Maintain high expectations for independent written work. *Fluency Foundations* written work should develop good work habits.

TEACH EXPECTATIONS FOR WRITTEN WORK

Explain and model expectations, then verify students' understanding with positive and negative examples.

It is important to do your best on your Comprehension and Skill Work. Doing your best means that you work carefully and check to make sure you do the following:

- Keep your paper flat, whole, and neat.
  What should your paper look like? (flat, whole, and neat)
  First, your paper should be flat.

  Show examples of a flat and crumpled paper.
  Point to the paper that is best.
  Next, your paper should be whole.

  Show examples of a whole paper and a torn paper.
  Point to the paper that is best.
  Your paper should be neat, without extra marks.

  Show examples of a paper with scribbles and one without scribbles.
  Point to the paper that is best.

- Your next job is to write as neatly as you can.
  Everyone will have a personal best in handwriting.
  Let's look at two of my papers. I worked carefully on one and not the other.

  Project two examples—an example of your personal best and a non-example. Have your students vote. Which paper do you think is the best? This one? Or this one?

  This is my personal best because the letters sit on the lines. The letters are formed correctly, and I have spaces between the words.

- Use capitals at the beginning of sentences and periods at the end of a sentence.

- Have students practice.
  Have students practice writing an answer to a written question.

- Provide gentle, supportive corrections.

- Acknowledge students' efforts and accomplishments.
  Provide each student with a sample of his or her own personal best to use as a reference. [Jonelle], you left a space between every word. Excellent. This paper goes in your folder as a sample of your personal best!

HANDWRITING

If students have difficulty with handwriting, add handwriting practice activities into your daily routine.

REVIEW EXPECTATIONS

Make a poster and have students periodically read the poem with you to review expectations.

I'LL DO MY BEST

I'll put myself to the test. I'll do my very best.

I'll keep my paper flat. I'll do it just like that.

I'll keep my paper whole. Oh, what a goal!

I'll keep my paper neat. My writing can't be beat.

I'll put myself to the test.

I'll always do my best.

Explicit Instruction · Comprehension and Skill Work

Preview the Comprehension and Skill directions in the teacher's guide before calling your small group. New skills are marked with a ★ in the teacher's guides and on the Comprehension and Skill Work.

When teaching Comprehension and Skill Work, apply the principles of explicit instruction. For each lesson, give students as much instruction as they need to be successful—but allow as much independence as possible.

Before teaching, preview the Comprehension and Skill lessons. Select one activity and practice with a colleague.

HOW TO TEACH COMPREHENSION AND SKILL WORK

For each Comprehension and Skill lesson, assess your students' skill level, then provide a demonstration, a guided practice, and/or independent practice, as appropriate.

- **To demonstrate:** Have the students respond while you write the answers on the page.

- **To guide students through the activity:** Have your students provide answers orally. Do not model the written answers.

- **To set students up for independent work:** Provide students with clear directions and support for independent work.

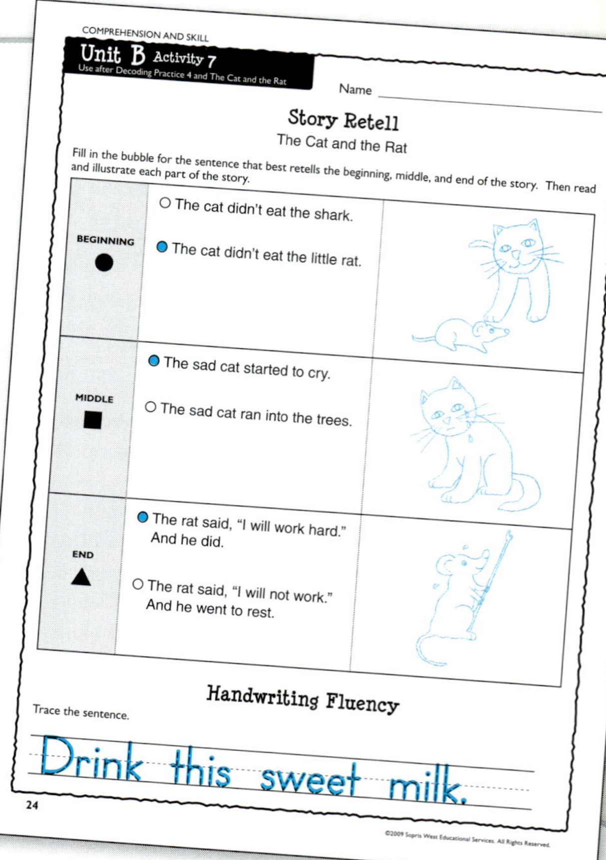

Unit B, Activity 7

CHECK AND CORRECT

Check all student work. Guide corrections at an appropriate time.

- Think aloud about the difficult answers. As appropriate, ask questions like: Does your answer make sense? Why not?

- Think aloud with students: That answer isn't the best because . . . Help students find the answer in their books: Let's look back.

Homework

In this section:

 **7.1 Materials and Routines**

Regular Reading Homework

- Builds connections with each child's school and home
- Provides manageable and successful reading experiences in the home
- Provides a vehicle for parents to applaud their child's progress
- Provides additional reading opportunities, building critical fluency foundations
- Provides an opportunity for parents and children to discuss reading passages
- Helps children develop a sense of responsibility

Materials and Routines

MATERIALS

- Blackline masters include a note to parents about participation, reprints of stories from Units A–J, and motivational charts.
- Copy homework, 1 double-sided reading folder per lesson.

COMMUNICATION AND POSITIVE INTERACTIONS

Explain the homework process to parents during conferences or through letters home. If a child is not having success with homework routines, have the child read to an older student or parent volunteer before going home. The child should still take his or her homework home and return it to school to help develop good homework habits.

To ensure positive interactions at home, homework for each unit should be sent home either during the unit or after the unit is completed. Do not send homework home in advance of instruction.

ROUTINES

To encourage regular reading habits, set up a routine agreed on by all grade level teachers. A suggested routine follows:

1. Assign *Read Well* homework Monday through Thursday, with each assignment due the following day.

2. Have reading teachers pass out homework during reading group. Homework should be placed in a homework folder.

3. To ensure that homework goes home, the homeroom teacher should have all students hold up their homework folders before they leave.

4. Each evening, students should read the stories to a parent or caregiver. Adults should date and sign each homework assignment and return it to school the next day.

5. Teachers should acknowledge students' efforts and periodically send a note of thanks to parents.

6. To keep accurate homework records, students should place their homework folders on the corner of their desks in the morning. As the homeroom teacher takes roll, homework completion can be quickly recorded.

7. When students go to their reading groups, they should take their homework folders with them. To ensure that the folders make it to the reading group, homeroom teachers should again ask all students to hold up their folders as part of their transition process.

"

End of the Unit

In this section:

8.1 **Assessments**

8.2 **Making Decisions**

Young students thrive when their lessons are supportive and successful. Because children have a range of background knowledge and respond to instruction differently, it is critical to deliver lessons that are tailored to their needs. At the end of each *Fluency Foundations* unit, you will monitor progress and adjust instruction, as appropriate.

Assessments

Research Snapshot

Ongoing Assessment

"Because the ability to obtain meaning from print depends so strongly on the development of word recognition accuracy and fluency, both the latter should be regularly assessed in the classroom, permitting timely and effective instructional response when difficulty or delay is apparent" (Snow, Burns, & Griffith, 1998, p. 7).

Assessment is vital to long-term reading health.

ORAL READING FLUENCY ASSESSMENTS

Regular assessment is an essential component of *Read Well.* The end-of-unit Oral Reading Fluency (ORF) Assessments are designed to frequently monitor progress while protecting instructional time. The timed assessment at the end of each unit takes only a couple of minutes per student and provides a quick, reliable checkup.

Fluency Foundations' Oral Reading Fluency Assessments will help you determine whether a child:

- is ready for the next unit and the addition of new skills.
- would benefit from Extra Practice lessons.
- needs a quick review to firm up past learning.
- would benefit from a slower pace of instruction.
- needs a faster pace of instruction.
- would benefit from instruction in a different group.

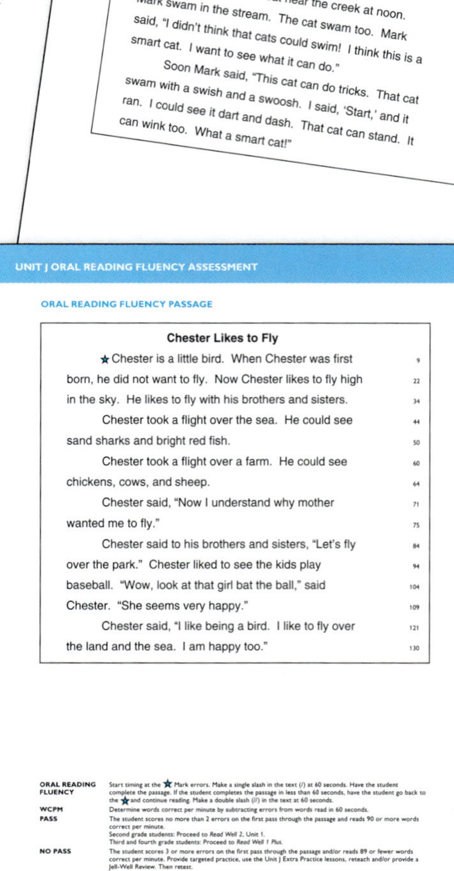

UNIT A ORAL READING FLUENCY ASSESSMENT

ORAL READING FLUENCY PASSAGE

A Sweet Dream

★ Mark had a sweet dream. In the dream, he had a neat cat.	
Mark and the cat sat near the creek at noon.	9
Mark swam in the stream. The cat swam too. Mark	13
said, "I didn't think that cats could swim! I think this is a	23
smart cat. I want to see what it can do."	33
Soon Mark said, "This cat can do tricks. That cat	46
swam with a swish and a swoosh. I said, 'Start,' and it	56
ran. I could see it dart and dash. That cat can stand. It	66
can wink too. What a smart cat!"	78
	91
	98

UNIT J ORAL READING FLUENCY ASSESSMENT

ORAL READING FLUENCY PASSAGE

Chester Likes to Fly

★ Chester is a little bird. When Chester was first	9
born, he did not want to fly. Now Chester likes to fly high	22
in the sky. He likes to fly with his brothers and sisters.	34
Chester took a flight over the sea. He could see	44
sand sharks and bright red fish.	50
Chester took a flight over a farm. He could see	60
chickens, cows, and sheep.	64
Chester said, "Now I understand why mother	71
wanted me to fly."	75
Chester said to his brothers and sisters, "Let's fly	84
over the park." Chester liked to see the kids play	94
baseball. "Wow, look at that girl bat the ball," said	104
Chester. "She seems very happy."	109
Chester said, "I like being a bird. I like to fly over	121
the land and the sea. I am happy too."	130

ORAL READING FLUENCY	Start timing at the ★ Mark errors. Make a single slash in the text (/) at 60 seconds. Have the student complete the passage. If the student completes the passage in less than 60 seconds, have the student go back to the ★ and continue reading. Make a double slash (//) in the text at 60 seconds.
WCPM	Determine words correct per minute by subtracting errors from words read in 60 seconds.
PASS	The student scores no more than 2 errors on the first pass through the passage and reads 90 or more words correct per minute. Second grade students: Proceed to *Read Well 2,* Unit 1. Third and fourth grade students: Proceed to *Read Well 1 Plus.*
NO PASS	The student scores 3 or more errors on the first pass through the passage and/or reads 89 or fewer words correct per minute. Provide targeted practice, use the Unit J Extra Practice lessons, reteach and/or provide a Jell-Well Review. Then retest.

292

Who Should Administer

Any trained professional (e.g., teacher, specialist, paraprofessional) can assess students.

When to Administer

Administer the Oral Reading Fluency Assessments on the last or next-to-last day of instruction in each unit. Assess the most fluent students first.

The Oral Reading Fluency Assessments can be administered while other students are working on Comprehension and Skill Work or while other students are reading with partners. The following variables can help teachers maintain ongoing assessment:

- Sufficient amounts of instructional time per group
  (See page 34 for a description of walk-to-read models.)
- A reading coach or floating paraprofessional to help assess individuals
- Trained volunteers who can work confidentially to assist with assessments

Materials Preparation

1. **Administration Form:** Make one copy of each end-of-unit Oral Reading Fluency Assessment for each person administering the assessments. Blackline masters are found in the Appendix of this manual.

2. **Scoring Forms:** Make a copy of each end-of-unit Oral Reading Fluency Assessment for each student. Blackline masters are found in the Appendix of this manual.

3. **Group Record Form:** Make a copy of the group record form or set up a similar computer database. A blackline master is found in the Appendix of this manual.

4. **Stop Watch:** Provide a stopwatch for each person administering the assessments.

Administration

ADMINISTERING THE END-OF-UNIT ASSESSMENT

- **Individually Administered:** Assess each student individually at a desk.

- **Warm-up:** As a warm-up, have the student read the title and predict what the passage will be about.

- **Timing:** Start timing the passage at the ★. Mark errors using the diagnostic scoring on page 99. Have the student complete the passage and continue reading for a full 60 seconds.

  - If the student has not completed the passage by the end of 60 seconds, make a single slash (/) after the last word read by the student. Have the student finish the passage.

  - If the student finishes the passage before 60 seconds have passed, have the student go back to the ★ and keep reading. Stop the student at 60 seconds and make a double slash (//) after the last word read by the student. On the second pass, mark errors differently (e.g. ✔).

- Record errors using the diagnostic scoring system on page 99.

UNIT G ORF ASSESSMENT	ADMINISTRATION AND SCORING

ORAL READING FLUENCY PASSAGE

Jonah   10/15
-3   90 WCPM

The Lost Ring

★I had a ring. [but] I lost it at the zoo. I asked   12

people, "Have you seen my ring?"   18

Alexander said, "I'm a detective! I will solve the   27

Case of the Missing Ring!"   32

Alexander and I went looking for my ring. We   41

made a list of where I had been. We looked near the   53

plants. We looked [near] in the weeds. My brother Zack   62

came up to me. He asked, "What are you doing?"   72

[search/look sc]
I said, "Alexander is helping me look for my ring.   82

He is a great detective."   87

[92 - 2 = 90 WCPM]
Zack said, "That is funny. / Did you forget? Your   96

ring is in your (zipper) pocket!"   102

Alexander said, "The case is solved!"   108

I was happy to have my ring back.   116

Doesn't want to finger track.
Errors are due to context cueing.

Had Jonah try reading two other paragraphs with and without finger tracking. Zero errors with finger tracking. Goal Setting and paragraph practice for accuracy

SCORING
Write student's name and date, mark any errors, and record total passage errors and WCPM on this page.

ORAL READING FLUENCY
Start timing at the ★. Mark errors. Make a single slash in the text (/) at 60 seconds. Have the student complete the passage. If the student completes the passage in less than 60 seconds, have the student go back to the ★ and continue reading. Make a double slash (//) in the text at 60 seconds.

WCPM
Determine words correct per minute by subtracting errors from words read in 60 seconds.

PASS
The student scores no more than 2 errors on the first pass through the passage and reads 82 or more words correct per minute. Proceed to Unit H.

NO PASS
The student scores 3 or more errors on the first pass through the passage and/or reads 81 or fewer words correct per minute. Provide targeted practice, use the Unit G Extra Practice lessons, reteach, and/or provide a Jell-Well Review. Then retest.

Diagnostic Scoring

DIAGNOSTIC SCORING		
If the student . . .	**Then . . .**	**Record . . .**
Needs Assistance	Wait three seconds. Gently tell the student the correct response, draw a line through the item, and write an "A" for "assisted." Score as an incorrect response.	Incorrect Alexander said, "I'm a detective." _(A written above, line through "Alexander")_
Mispronounces or Substitutes Word or Sound	Draw a line through the word. Record what the student said. Score as an incorrect response.	Incorrect Alexander and I went looking for the ring. _(were written above "went")_
Omits a Word or Word Part	Circle the omission. Score as an incorrect response.	Incorrect My brother Zack came (up) to me.
Inserts a Word	Write what the student said, using a caret to show where the student inserted the word. Score as incorrect.	Incorrect Zack said, "That is ^funny." _(very written above caret)_
Self-Corrects	If the student spontaneously self-corrects, write "SC" and score as a correct response. If the student requires more than two attempts, score as an incorrect response.	Correct Your ring is in your zipper pocket. _(my/your and sc written above "your")_ Incorrect Your ring is in your zipper pocket. _(my/you/your written above "your")_
Repeats a Word	Underline repeated words. Score as a correct response.	Correct <u>Alexander</u> said, "The case is solved."
Reverses Words	Draw a line around the words as shown. Score as a correct response.	Correct I was happy to have my ring back. _(line drawn around "ring back")_

SECOND TIME THROUGH		
Any Error	Make a ✓ over each word.	✓ I'm a detective.

Making Decisions

Research Snapshot

Oral Reading Fluency

Research has shown that oral reading fluency can be a stronger measure of comprehension than traditionally used classroom assessments for reading comprehension. Fuchs, Fuchs, and Maxwell (1988) found a significantly higher correlation between oral reading fluency and the Comprehension Subtest of the Stanford Reading Achievement Test than between fluency and traditional direct measures of comprehension (e.g., question answering, passage recall, and cloze).

With *Read Well*, every teacher is a diagnostician. It is important to keep track of error patterns and reteach any difficult words or skills. Prescriptions for placement, pacing, and instruction are provided in each unit's teacher's guide.

Pass, No Pass

In *Fluency Foundations*, you will find the criteria for a Pass and No Pass at the bottom of each assessment.

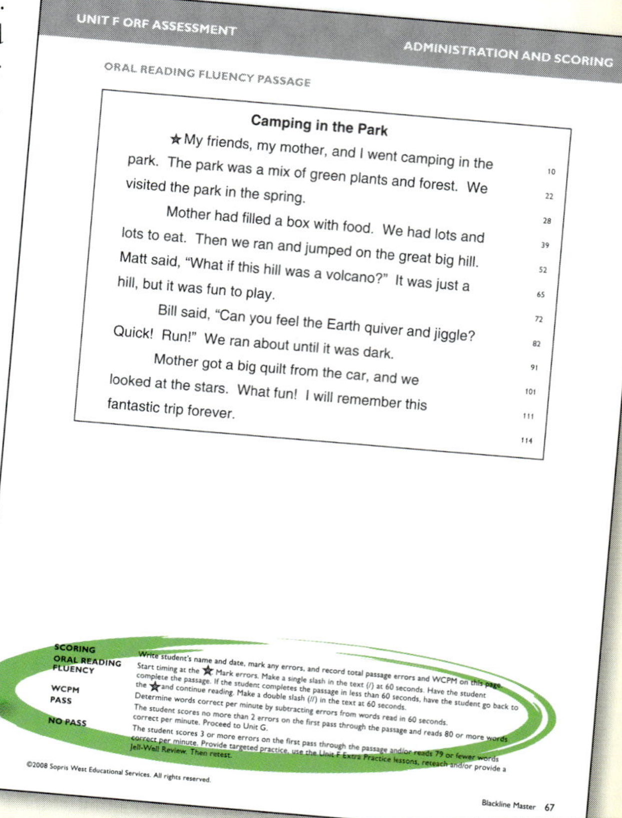

PASS	The student scores no more than 2 errors on the first pass through the passage and reads 80 or more words correct per minute. Proceed to Unit G.
NO PASS	The student scores 3 or more errors on the first pass through the passage and/or reads 79 or fewer words correct per minute. Provide targeted practice, use the Unit F Extra Practice lessons, reteach and/or provide a Jell-Well Review. Then retest.

Acceleration

If a group is reading with a high degree of fluency, a faster pace of instruction may be warranted. If students are reading 25 to 30 words correct per minute above the Pass WCPM with 0–2 errors, shorten the length of the unit from 4 to 3 days.

When an individual student excels, regrouping should be considered.

WCPM Progression

Unit	No Pass WCPM	Pass WCPM and	Acceleration WCPM* and
A	54 or fewer	**55** or more	85
B	59 or fewer	**60** or more	85
C	64 or fewer	**65** or more	90
D	69 or fewer	**70** or more	95
E	74 or fewer	**75** or more	100
F	79 or fewer	**80** or more	105
G	81 or fewer	**82** or more	105
H	84 or fewer	**85** or more	110
I	87 or fewer	**88** or more	110
J	89 or fewer	**90** or more	—

***If the entire group is achieving the Acceleration WCPM, try the 3-Day Plan.**

Pass

Continue with the current pace of instruction. Consider increasing fluency practice. Some students will need more practice than others in the group to build and maintain fluency, even though they may be reading accurately. Prescriptions include short tutorials and/or a second dose of reading.

No Pass

Errors indicate a need to reteach. However, some teacher discretion is required. If errors are the result of a repeated mistake on a single word or skill, it is appropriate to move forward but reteach the word or skill. Some students have a firm understanding of skills but are careless with reading. Sometimes an increased focus on accuracy will suffice.

Added Practice Options

The Making Decisions section provides prescriptions that include Extra Practice lessons to extend units and/or a Jell-Well Review of earlier units.

Adjusting Instruction

At the end of each unit, record scores on your Group ORF Assessment Record. (A blackline master of this form is in the Appendix.) If you are part of a walk-to-read model, meet on a regular basis to share results, problem solve, and regroup, as appropriate. When regrouping, watch for trends. Do not rely on a single score.

GENERAL PRESCRIPTIONS		
When . . .	**Scores a . . .**	**Then . . .**
An entire small group	25 to 30 words correct per minute above a Pass	Consider a faster pace of instruction. If the group is on a 4-day core plan, drop to a 3-day plan.
Individuals within a small group		Consider moving those individuals into a higher-level group.
An entire small group	Pass	Continue forward at the same pace of instruction.
An entire small group Individuals within a small group	No Pass	Emphasize instruction and practice on any difficult skills while: • providing Extra Practice lessons for the unit. • reteaching lessons or the unit. • previewing the next unit. • providing a Jell-Well Review of previous units (see page 108). Provide a second dose of instruction for these students. Consider regrouping.

PASS

Most students will receive Passes when:

• placed appropriately.
• grouped appropriately.
• given sufficient instructional time.
• taught well.

Adjusting Instruction

Group ORF Assessment Record

Record student scores on the Group Assessment Record. (A blackline master is found in the Appendix.)

Analyze student scores to:

- determine whether students are ready to move forward or would benefit from Extra Practice lessons
- track the progress of individual students
- compare the progress of individual students within the group
- quickly share assessment results with colleagues
- make regrouping decisions

Example

Ms. Pierce has coded her Assessment Record as follows:

- A circle indicates a No Pass due to errors or rate.
- Numbers with a slash indicate reteaching and a retest.

Diagnostic Prescriptive Teaching

In Unit A, eight students fail the assessment due to errors. Ms. Pierce analyzes the errors: "sweet" for "neat," "cat" for "cats," "the" for "this," "that" for "this," "that" for "what."

Ms. Pierce notes that errors are due to using context to determine words and reading by sight. In general, Ms. Pierce determines that her students need to learn to discriminate words that begin with w-h and those that begin with t-h. Ms. Pierce follows the prescriptions on pages 104–106 of this guide for increasing accuracy and correcting errors on Tricky Words.

Extra Practice

Ms. Pierce uses Extra Practice lessons to reteach Unit A. During these lessons, she targets reading for accuracy and discrimination of words that begin with t-h and w-h. On retesting, all eight students pass.

Double Dosing/Jell-Well Review

By Unit E, Ms. Pierce sees that Jamal, Ming, Darren, and Mary have each had three or four No Passes. Ms. Pierce decides to explore options for additional practice. She finds that an AmeriCorps volunteer is available three days each week to listen to the students read. Jamal, Ming, Darren, and Mary are set up for 15-minute one-to-one tutorials. Ms. Pierce decides to have the students do a Jell-Well Review (a systematic review of earlier units). Students will go back to Unit B with the AmeriCorps volunteer. During the 15-minute sessions, they will do Extra Practice Decoding and Passage Reading.

Fluency Foundations Group ORF Assessment Record

INSTRUCTOR: Ms. Pierce

Unit		Goal	A		B		C		D		E	
Assessment Date			9-15/9-22		9-30		10-6		10-15		10-21	
Pass (WCPM)			55	0–2	60	0–2	65	0–2	70	0–2	75	0–2
Acceleration			85		85		90		95		100	
			WCPM / ERRORS		WCPM / ERRORS		WCPM / ERRORS		WCPM / ERRORS		WCPM / ERRORS	
1.	Ruben	(70/4)	70/77	(5)/1	78	2	80	0	86	0	79	0
2.	Sally	(67/3)	(53)/75	(5)/1	74	2	83	1	91	2	94	0
3.	Allie	(65/4)	63/67	(6)/2	81	2	75	0	78	2	83	2
4.	Jamal	(63/3)	59	1	(54)/60	1/2	Ab		(69)/73	1/(3)	(74)/75	0/1
5.	Chau	(62/3)	64/91	(5)/2	66	2	(64)/67	1/2	78	2	82	2
6.	Benje	(61/4)	(54)/76	(5)/2	72	2	70	2	(65)(69)/	1/0	75	2
7.	Hailey	(59/2)	56/66	(3)/2	68	1	72	1	(58)/73	2/0	(74)/79	1/0
8.	Ming	(58/2)	56	2	(53)(59)/	0/2	(64)/65	2/1	(57)/75	0/1	(63)/75	1/0
9.	Darren	(56/3)	58/71	(3)/2	72	1	(63)/70	0/0	(58)/70	1/0	(71)/78	2/2
10.	Michael	(56/2)	56	2	(58)/61	2/1	67	2	77	0	82	0
11.	Mary	(55/0)	71/77	(5)/2	75	0	68	0	(65)/73	0/2	(73)/77	0/2
12.												
13.												
14.												
15.												

Comments
Unit A · Added 3 days Extra Practice due to errors, much better
Unit B · 6-day plan, errors down
Unit C · Chau had a cold, watch Ming and Darren
Unit D · Added 2 extra days Extra Practice rested
Unit E · Add tutorials for Jamal, Ming, Darren, Mary—Jell Well

Blackline Master 97

Diagnostic-Prescriptive Teaching

With *Read Well*, every teacher is a diagnostician. Analyze errors, watch for patterns, reteach as needed, and provide focused instruction and practice.

SPECIFIC PRESCRIPTIONS	
If students have difficulty with . . .	**Then try these prescriptions . . .**
Reading accurately	Focus on reducing careless errors, repetitions, and self-corrections during oral reading. Follow these steps:

1. Provide an Extra Practice lesson. (*Fluency Foundations* and *Read Well 1* correlations are found in the teacher's guides in the Sequence and Sound Pronunciation Guides and also in this manual on page 7.)

   a. After students read the passage, have children listen to you read. Tell students that they can raise their hands (or mark their stories with a simple slash) when they hear you make an error. Model each of the following types of errors:
      - Reading a word incorrectly
      - Leaving out a word

   Explain that it is important to read words accurately and only once. Tell students they should also count the following as errors:
      - Making corrections
      - Repeating a word

   b. Read the passage slowly. Make errors and ham it up. The children will love catching your errors.

   c. Have students read the passage with individual turns on sentences. Quietly count errors.

   d. Review the errors without identifying individuals. Have students practice reading the sentences accurately.

   e. Have students reread the passage. The goal is to improve students' accuracy.

   f. Acknowledge accomplishments. Say things like: Wow, you read two paragraphs carefully.

2. Give students individual turns when they finger track. Say things like: [Jack], you get to read the next two sentences. You had your finger on the words, and you are reading each word carefully.

3. Have students set group and individual goals. Say things like: You read page 13 with only two mistakes—*the* instead of *a* and *walk* instead of *walking.* Do you think we can read the next page with only one mistake?

Diagnostic-Prescriptive Teaching

SPECIFIC PRESCRIPTIONS	
If students have difficulty with . . .	**Then try these prescriptions . . .**
Pattern Words	Provide gentle immediate corrections, identify error patterns, and firm up underlying skill deficits. Follow these steps: 1. To correct common errors (e.g., reading "man" for "men," "sleep" for "slept," or "hot" for "hat"), have the group identify the missed sound, then sound out the word. For minimal pairs, put both words on the board. Error: A student or students read "plan" for "plain." • Have students identify the missed sound. There was one sound that tricked some of us. **Point to the sound.** Tell me the sound. (/āāā/) • Have students sound out the word with the correct sound. Sound out the word smoothly. (plllāāānnn) Read the word. (plain) The opposite of fancy is . . . (plain). That's right. That hat is not fancy. It is . . . plain. • Practice other words. Return to the difficult word at least three times. • Acknowledge student responses. You know the difference between *plan* and *plain*. 2. Word Practice: Identify any commonly missed sounds. For example if students read "man" for "men" and "want" for "went," they haven't mastered the short vowel e. Add an extra list of short vowel e words into daily practice. Underline the e. Have students read the underlined sounds first, and then the words. 3. Sound Practice: Add extra practice with any difficult sound. If the short vowel e is difficult, add additional short vowel e cards to Sound Card Practice.
Tricky Words	1. To correct common errors (e.g., reading "what" for "that," "where" for "there," or "and" for "said"), have the group orally spell the word with letter names. For minimal pairs such as errors on "where" and "were," emphasize the letter that makes the difference. For example, write "wHere" on the board. Have the group orally spell "where," saying the letter H loudly. Then have students write three questions with "where." Repeat practice each day.

Have students correct the error.

Critical step

Diagnostic-Prescriptive Teaching

SPECIFIC PRESCRIPTIONS	
If students have difficulty with . . .	**Then try these prescriptions . . .**
Tricky Words (continued)	2. Have students practice reading the Tricky Words on the back of their Homework on a daily basis. Do not have *Fluency Foundations* students practice from generic high-frequency word lists. High-frequency words are taught in sequence with the sounds taught. High-frequency words—irregular words—are introduced gradually and within the letter/sound sequence, even though irregular.

Fluency
 	
Appropriate practice makes perfect.
	1. Extend lessons (e.g., if students are working on 6-Day Plans, implement 8-Day Plans). Spend more time on repeated readings of stories.
	  • After practicing the story with choral reading and individual turns on sentences, give each student a turn to read a page.
	  • Set an accuracy goal of 0–2 errors.
	  • To motivate practice, give each student a transparency and a marker. Have students follow along and mark errors as individuals take turns.
	  • Have the strongest reader read first. Model giving compliments.
	  • Have one or two students give a compliment to each child.
	  • Congratulate the child each time his or her fluency improves.
	
	2. Set up extra reading sessions with a tutor.
	  • Set an accuracy goal of 0–2 errors.
	  • Have the student read a previously read *Read Well* Homework story for accuracy or have the student read correlated *Read Well 1* stories. (*Fluency Foundations* and *Read Well 1* correlations are found in the teacher's guides in the Sequence and Sound Pronunciation Guides and also in this manual on page 7.)
	
	3. Set up Fluency Booster Notebooks that include previously read homework stories. Put the stories in three-ring binders. Begin each day's lesson with a three-minute Whisper Read from the old homework stories. Have students mark where they are at the end of three minutes. The next day, the goal is to read farther. *Read Well 1* homework can also be used when correlated with the *Fluency Foundations* units.
	
	5. Have students read into a tape recorder. Then have them listen to their reading and mark errors on a transparency. Have the student reread until satisfied with his or her recording.
	
	6. Provide additional Short Passage Practice with individuals.
	  • Model how to read a paragraph teith expression.
	  • Reread the paragraph with the student.
	  • Have the student reread the paragraph.

Extra Practice

Most children can benefit from extra practice, but some children *require* extra practice to master new skills with depth and fluency.

Each *Fluency Foundations* unit includes four Extra Practice lessons. Each lesson is composed of teacher-directed decoding practice and fluency practice as well as independent work. For ease in planning, the Extra Practice lessons are incorporated into the 6- and 8-Day Lesson Plans. These lessons (all or in part) may also be used in tutorials or in double dosing for students who need additional fluency practice.

EXTRA PRACTICE COMPONENTS

Decoding Practice

Extra Practice targets:

Sound Review: Review of vowels

Sounding Out Smoothly: Blending sounds into words

Accuracy and Fluency Building: Automatic recognition of common letter sounds, vowel discrimination, and affixes

Tricky Words: High-frequency irregular words

Multisyllabic Words: Reading recognizable chunks from left to right

Dictation: Letter sound associations and onsets and rimes

Fluency Passages

Each Extra Practice lesson includes fluency passages to build accuracy, fluency, and prosody.

Activities

Each Extra Practice lesson includes a Comprehension and Skill Activity designed to build story comprehension.

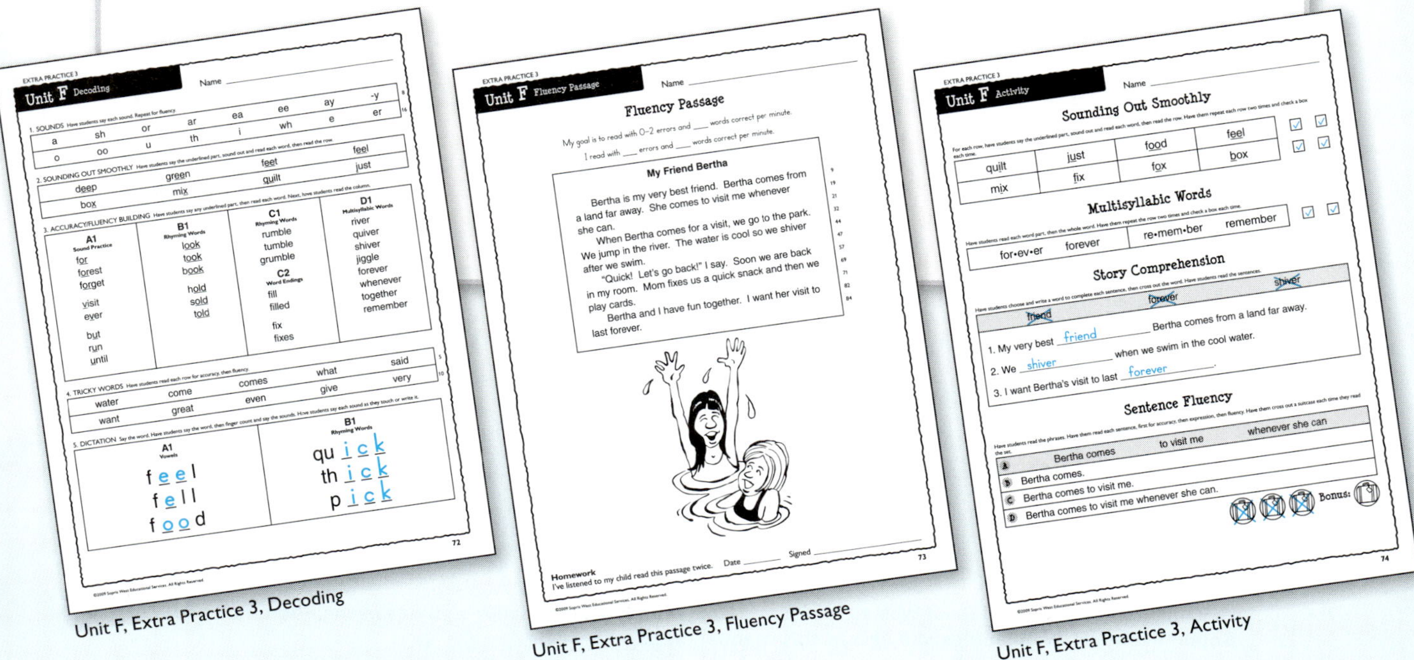

Unit F, Extra Practice 3, Decoding

Unit F, Extra Practice 3, Fluency Passage

Unit F, Extra Practice 3, Activity

Intervention and Jell-Well Reviews

Extra Practice

The flow chart demonstrates how to plan instruction based on student performance and extend practice as needed with each unit's Extra Practice lessons.

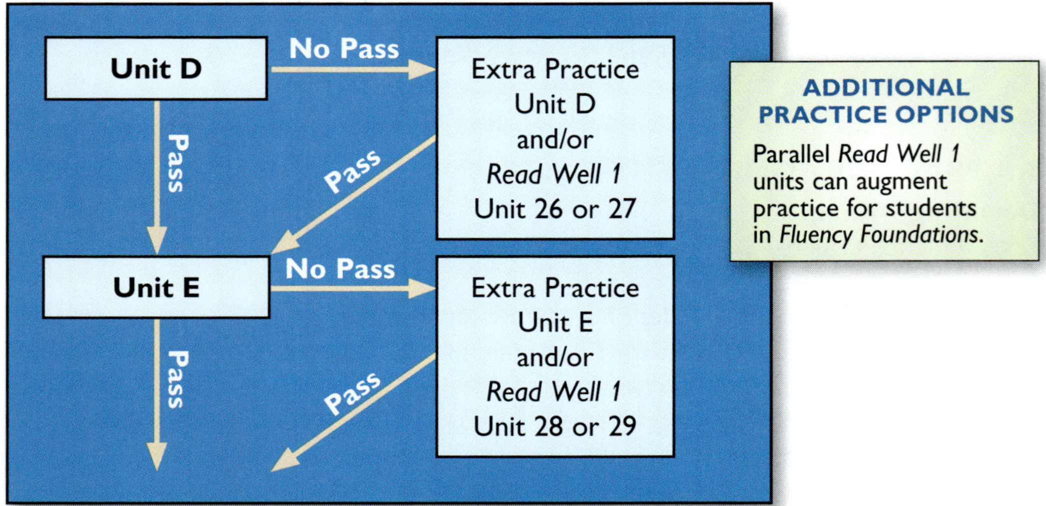

Jell-Well Review

Jell-Well Review is the *Read Well* term for a review of earlier units. A Jell-Well Review is a period of time taken to celebrate what children have learned and an opportunity to firm up their foundation of learning.

Why Is a Jell-Well Needed?

Fluency Foundations is a fast-paced review of skills introduced in *Read Well 1*. If your students had *Read Well 1* in First Grade and did not complete *Read Well 1* with mastery, the latter units may require more time for mastery.

Jell-Well Reviews are sometimes needed for the lowest performers in a group. When there is a range in a group, the lowest-performing students need the most practice. Unfortunately, these students often end up taking a back seat during lessons and so get the least amount of practice. When this occurs, a gentle review and added practice sessions are often necessary to close the gap. When there is a range of fluency levels in a group, the lowest-performing students will require more practice.

How to Do Jell-Well Reviews

Find the last unit in which the student or students had a Strong Pass. Start the Jell-Well Review with the next unit. For example, in Mr. York's group, Cody received a No Pass in Units B, C, D, and E. Jell-Well Reviews can be conducted by using Extra Practice lessons, recycling through previously taught core lessons, or by using the related *Read Well 1* materials.

***Fluency Foundations and Read Well 1 correlations are found in the teacher's guides in the Sequence and Sound Pronunciation Guides and also in this manual on page 7.**

Appendix

In this section:

- Zoom, Zoom, Zoom!
- Lesson Planner
- Double Dose Lesson Planner
- *Read Well 2* Placement Test
- *Read Well 2* Student Placement Record
- *Read Well 2* Group Placement Form
- *Fluency Foundations* Group ORF Assessment Record
- *Fluency Foundations* Individual ORF Assessment Record
- Unit A–J ORF Assessments, Administration, and Scoring
- Selected References

Name _______________________________

I'm on the move
with *Fluency Foundations!*

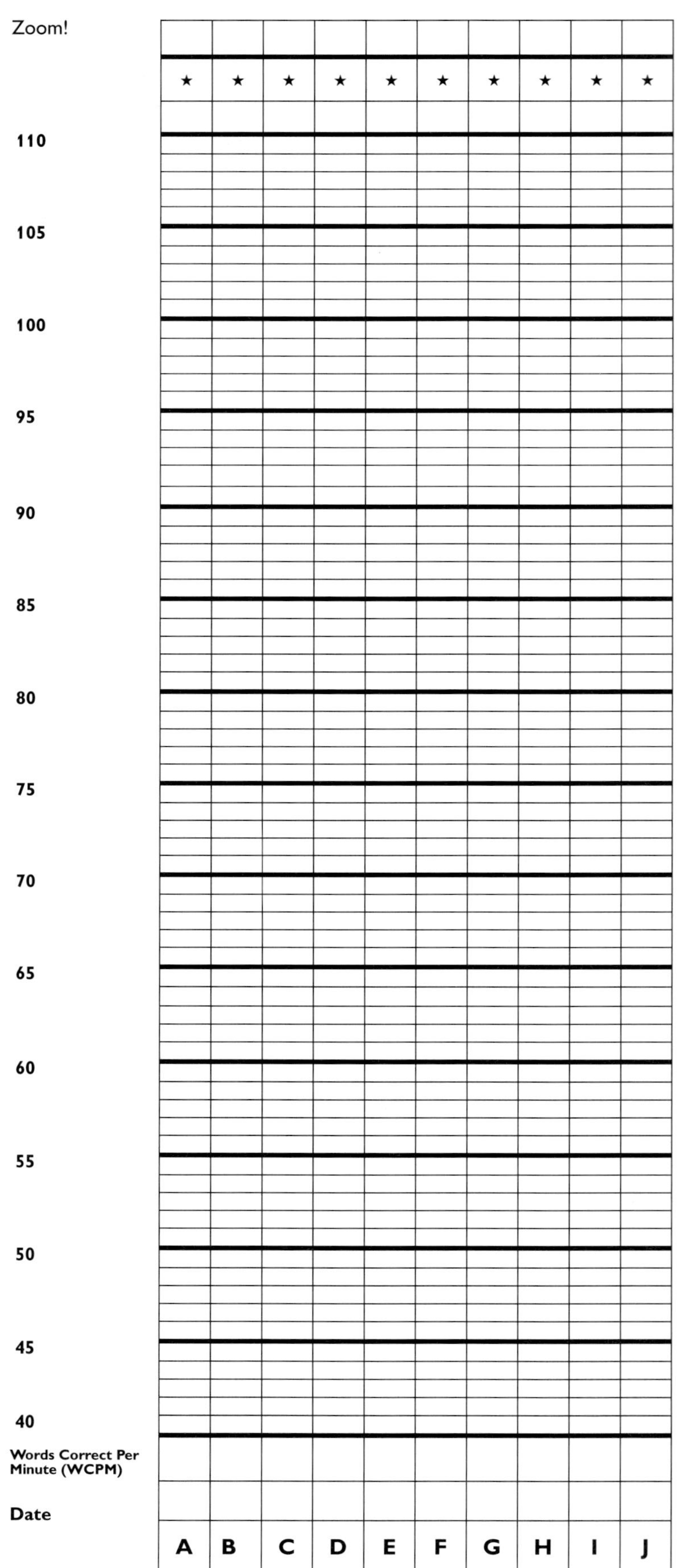

LESSON PLANNER

Month _________________ Grade _________ Instructor: _____________________________ *READ WELL* _________________

Monday	Tuesday	Wednesday	Thursday	Friday	Notes
Unit _______	**Unit** _______	**Unit** _______	**Unit** _______	**Unit** _______	____________
___ Decoding _______	___ Decoding _______	___ Decoding _______	___ Decoding _______	___ Decoding _______	____________
___ Story _______	___ Story _______	___ Story _______	___ Story _______	___ Story _______	____________
___ Comp/Skill _______	___ Comp/Skill _______	___ Comp/Skill _______	___ Comp/Skill _______	___ Comp/Skill _______	____________
___ Partner Rdg _______	___ Partner Rdg _______	___ Partner Rdg _______	___ Partner Rdg _______	___ Partner Rdg _______	____________
___ Assessment _______	___ Assessment _______	___ Assessment _______	___ Assessment _______	___ Assessment _______	____________
Unit _______	**Unit** _______	**Unit** _______	**Unit** _______	**Unit** _______	____________
___ Decoding _______	___ Decoding _______	___ Decoding _______	___ Decoding _______	___ Decoding _______	____________
___ Story _______	___ Story _______	___ Story _______	___ Story _______	___ Story _______	____________
___ Comp/Skill _______	___ Comp/Skill _______	___ Comp/Skill _______	___ Comp/Skill _______	___ Comp/Skill _______	____________
___ Partner Rdg _______	___ Partner Rdg _______	___ Partner Rdg _______	___ Partner Rdg _______	___ Partner Rdg _______	____________
___ Assessment _______	___ Assessment _______	___ Assessment _______	___ Assessment _______	___ Assessment _______	____________
Unit _______	**Unit** _______	**Unit** _______	**Unit** _______	**Unit** _______	____________
___ Decoding _______	___ Decoding _______	___ Decoding _______	___ Decoding _______	___ Decoding _______	____________
___ Story _______	___ Story _______	___ Story _______	___ Story _______	___ Story _______	____________
___ Comp/Skill _______	___ Comp/Skill _______	___ Comp/Skill _______	___ Comp/Skill _______	___ Comp/Skill _______	____________
___ Partner Rdg _______	___ Partner Rdg _______	___ Partner Rdg _______	___ Partner Rdg _______	___ Partner Rdg _______	____________
___ Assessment _______	___ Assessment _______	___ Assessment _______	___ Assessment _______	___ Assessment _______	____________
Unit _______	**Unit** _______	**Unit** _______	**Unit** _______	**Unit** _______	____________
___ Decoding _______	___ Decoding _______	___ Decoding _______	___ Decoding _______	___ Decoding _______	____________
___ Story _______	___ Story _______	___ Story _______	___ Story _______	___ Story _______	____________
___ Comp/Skill _______	___ Comp/Skill _______	___ Comp/Skill _______	___ Comp/Skill _______	___ Comp/Skill _______	____________
___ Partner Rdg _______	___ Partner Rdg _______	___ Partner Rdg _______	___ Partner Rdg _______	___ Partner Rdg _______	____________
___ Assessment _______	___ Assessment _______	___ Assessment _______	___ Assessment _______	___ Assessment _______	____________

DOUBLE DOSE LESSON PLANNER

Month ______ Grade ______ Instructor ______ *READ WELL*

Teacher

Monday	Tuesday	Wednesday	Thursday	Friday	Notes
Unit ___	Unit ___	Unit ___	Unit ___	Unit ___	
Decoding ___	Decoding ___	Decoding ___	Decoding ___	Decoding ___	
Story ___	Story ___	Story ___	Story ___	Story ___	
Comp/Skill ___	Comp/Skill ___	Comp/Skill ___	Comp/Skill ___	Comp/Skill ___	
Partner Rdg ___	Partner Rdg ___	Partner Rdg ___	Partner Rdg ___	Partner Rdg ___	
Assessment ___	Assessment ___	Assessment ___	Assessment ___	Assessment ___	
Unit ___	Unit ___	Unit ___	Unit ___	Unit ___	
Decoding ___	Decoding ___	Decoding ___	Decoding ___	Decoding ___	
Story ___	Story ___	Story ___	Story ___	Story ___	
Comp/Skill ___	Comp/Skill ___	Comp/Skill ___	Comp/Skill ___	Comp/Skill ___	
Partner Rdg ___	Partner Rdg ___	Partner Rdg ___	Partner Rdg ___	Partner Rdg ___	
Assessment ___	Assessment ___	Assessment ___	Assessment ___	Assessment ___	

Teacher

Monday	Tuesday	Wednesday	Thursday	Friday	Notes
Unit ___	Unit ___	Unit ___	Unit ___	Unit ___	
Decoding ___	Decoding ___	Decoding ___	Decoding ___	Decoding ___	
Story ___	Story ___	Story ___	Story ___	Story ___	
Comp/Skill ___	Comp/Skill ___	Comp/Skill ___	Comp/Skill ___	Comp/Skill ___	
Partner Rdg ___	Partner Rdg ___	Partner Rdg ___	Partner Rdg ___	Partner Rdg ___	
Assessment ___	Assessment ___	Assessment ___	Assessment ___	Assessment ___	
Unit ___	Unit ___	Unit ___	Unit ___	Unit ___	
Decoding ___	Decoding ___	Decoding ___	Decoding ___	Decoding ___	
Story ___	Story ___	Story ___	Story ___	Story ___	
Comp/Skill ___	Comp/Skill ___	Comp/Skill ___	Comp/Skill ___	Comp/Skill ___	
Partner Rdg ___	Partner Rdg ___	Partner Rdg ___	Partner Rdg ___	Partner Rdg ___	
Assessment ___	Assessment ___	Assessment ___	Assessment ___	Assessment ___	

TRICKY WORD WARM-UP

does	only	water	boy	gone

ORAL READING FLUENCY PASSAGE

Take Flight, Little Bird

★Chester was a little bird who did not want to fly. His mother   13
said, "Take flight, Chester. You might like it. Look at your brother   25
and sisters. They are having such fun flying high in the sky."   37

Chester said, "It doesn't sound like fun to me."   46

Then one day, Chester's mother told him, "It's getting cold. We   57
must go south for the winter."   63

Chester said, "Not me. I'm staying put."   70

Soon the other birds left. When night fell, Chester was all alone.   82

Suddenly Chester shouted, "Wait for me!"   88

Chester's mother was waiting nearby. She smiled and said,   97
"That's my boy!"   100

ORAL READING FLUENCY   Start timing at the ★. Mark errors. Make a single slash in the text (/) at 60 seconds.
If the student completes the passage in less than 60 seconds, have the student go back to the ★
and continue reading. Make a double slash (//) in the text at 60 seconds.

See the Student Placement Record for placement prescriptions (pages 114).

IMPORTANT: Follow the scoring and recording procedures shown on pages 30 and 31. For each unit, check the student's pass level.

NAME ____

TEACHER ____

	READ WELL 2 INITIAL PLACEMENT TEST	SCORE/COMMENTS
Tricky Word Warm-Up	does only water boy gone	

Oral Reading Fluency Passage	**Take Flight Little Bird**		
	★Chester was a little bird who did not want to fly. His mother	13	
	said, "Take flight, Chester. You might like it. Look at your brother	25	Accuracy: ______
	and sisters. They are having such fun flying high in the sky."	37	Passage Errors
	Chester said, "It doesn't sound like fun to me."	46	
	Then one day, Chester's mother told him, "It's getting cold. We	57	
	must go south for the winter."	63	Fluency: ______ WCPM
	Chester said, "Not me. I'm staying put."	70	(______ words read –
	Soon the other birds left. When night fell, Chester was all alone.	82	______ errors/minute)
	Suddenly Chester shouted, "Wait for me!"	88	
	Chester's mother was waiting nearby. She smiled and said,	97	
	"That's my boy!"	100	

Assessment Date(s): Check student score and placement/next step

  ___ No more than 3 errors and 55–79 words correct per minute: Place in *Fluency Foundations* Unit A.

  ___ 4 or more errors and/or 54 or fewer words correct per minute: Administer the Read Well 1 Placement Inventory.

Consider placement in *Read Well Plus* or *Read Well 2*.

  ___ No more than 3 errors and 80–99 words correct per minute: Place in *Read Well 2* Unit 1 or *Read Well 1 Plus* Unit 39.

  ___ No more than 3 errors and 100 or more words correct per minute: Administer the next step in the *Read Well 2* Assessment System.

DATE _______________________________ TEACHER(S) _______________________________

STUDENT NAME	Group	Possible In-Program Placement	WCPM Initial Placement Test	Errors Initial Placement Test	Comments

INSTRUCTOR: ____

Unit	A		B		C		D		E	
Assessment Date										
Goal Pass	WCPM 55	ERRORS 0–2	WCPM 60	ERRORS 0–2	WCPM 65	ERRORS 0–2	WCPM 70	ERRORS 0–2	WCPM 75	ERRORS 0–2
Acceleration	85		85		90		95		100	
1.										
2.										
3.										
4.										
5.										
6.										
7.										
8.										
9.										
10.										
11.										
12.										
13.										
14.										
15.										

INSTRUCTOR: ____

Unit		F		G		H		I		J	
Assessment Date											
Goal		WCPM	ERRORS	WCPM	ERRORS	WCPM	ERRORS	WCPM	ERRORS	WCPM	ERRORS
	Pass	80	0–2	82	0–2	85	0–2	88	0–2	90	0–2
	Acceleration	105		105		110		110		—	
1.											
2.											
3.											
4.											
5.											
6.											
7.											
8.											
9.											
10.											
11.											
12.											
13.											
14.											
15.											

NAME: _______________________________

Oral Reading Fluency Assessments

Unit	Date	Pass	Acceleration	Accuracy Score	ORF Score (WCPM)	Comments
A		55+	85			
B		60+	85			
C		65+	90			
D		70+	95			
E		75+	100			
F		80+	105			
G		82+	105			
H		85+	110			
I		88+	110			
J		90+	—			

ORAL READING FLUENCY PASSAGE

A Sweet Dream

★Mark had a sweet dream. In the dream, he had a neat cat.

Mark and the cat sat near the creek at noon. Mark swam in the stream. The cat swam too. Mark said, "I didn't think that cats could swim! I think this is a smart cat. I want to see what it can do."

Soon Mark said, "This cat can do tricks. That cat swam with a swish and a swoosh. I said, 'Start,' and it ran. I could see it dart and dash. That cat can stand. It can wink too. What a smart cat!"

SCORING	Write student's name and date, mark any errors, and record total passage errors and WCPM on this page.
ORAL READING FLUENCY	Start timing at the ★. Mark errors. Make a single slash in the text (/) at 60 seconds. Have the student complete the passage. If the student completes the passage in less than 60 seconds, have the student go back to the ★ and continue reading. Make a double slash (//) in the text at 60 seconds.
WCPM	Determine words correct per minute by subtracting errors from words read in 60 seconds.
PASS	The student scores no more than 2 errors on the first pass through the passage and reads 55 or more words correct per minute. Proceed to Unit B.
NO PASS	The student scores 3 or more errors on the first pass through the passage and/or reads 54 or fewer words correct per minute. Provide targeted practice, use the Unit A Extra Practice lessons, and/or reteach. Then retest.

ORAL READING FLUENCY PASSAGE

Shy Rick

★Rick was a shy little raccoon. When Rick was   9

one, he met Kim. Kim was a raccoon too. She was   20

three. Kim said, "Who is this raccoon?"   27

"I am Rick," said the shy raccoon.   34

Then Kim said, "I want to eat."   41

Rick said, "Me too. When can we eat? What can   51

we eat?"   53

Kim and Rick could smell a ham. It was in the   64

trash. Kim said, "Let's eat that ham."   71

A man was near. He said, "Who is there? Who   81

is in the trash?" Then he said, "Scat!"   89

Kim and Rick ran with the ham. "Tee hee," said   99

Rick and Kim.   102

SCORING	Write student's name and date, mark any errors, and record total passage errors and WCPM on this page.
ORAL READING FLUENCY	Start timing at the ★. Mark errors. Make a single slash in the text (/) at 60 seconds. Have the student complete the passage. If the student completes the passage in less than 60 seconds, have the student go back to the ★ and continue reading. Make a double slash (//) in the text at 60 seconds.
WCPM	Determine words correct per minute by subtracting errors from words read in 60 seconds.
PASS	The student scores no more than 2 errors on the first pass through the passage and reads 60 or more words correct per minute. Proceed to Unit C.
NO PASS	The student scores 3 or more errors on the first pass through the passage and/or reads 59 or fewer words correct per minute. Provide targeted practice, use the Unit B Extra Practice lessons, and/or reteach.

ORAL READING FLUENCY PASSAGE

A Grand Team

★It was hard work to be on the team with the   11

Tenth Street Bobcats. The Bobcats ran and ran. The   20

team hit and hit. The Bobcats worked and worked.   29

Beth said, "We should try and be the best team   39

we can be."   42

Matt said, "We need to be strong. Then we can   52

whack and blast that ball."   57

Rod said, "The Tenth Street Bobcats can swing   65

the bat, smack the ball, and win, win, win!"   74

Ann nodded and began to grin. Then she said,   83

"Isn't this a fantastic team?"   88

The team all said, "Go Bobcats! Let's blast that   97

ball!" What a grand team.   102

SCORING	Write student's name and date, mark any errors, and record total passage errors and WCPM on this page.
ORAL READING FLUENCY	Start timing at the ★. Mark errors. Make a single slash in the text (/) at 60 seconds. Have the student complete the passage. If the student completes the passage in less than 60 seconds, have the student go back to the ★ and continue reading. Make a double slash (//) in the text at 60 seconds.
WCPM	Determine words correct per minute by subtracting errors from words read in 60 seconds.
PASS	The student scores no more than 2 errors on the first pass through the passage and reads 65 or more words correct per minute. Proceed to Unit D.
NO PASS	The student scores 3 or more errors on the first pass through the passage and/or reads 64 or fewer words correct per minute. Provide targeted practice, use the Unit C Extra Practice lessons, reteach, and/or provide a Jell-Well Review. Then retest.

ORAL READING FLUENCY PASSAGE

Brothers

★Martin and Bob are brothers. Martin and Bob	8
do different things together.	12
Bob is too little to read, but his big brother reads	23
to him. Bob asks his big brother Martin, "What's this?	33
What's that? When? Where? Why?"	38
At noon, Bob and Martin went fishing. When	46
Bob and Martin were near the stream, Bob asked,	55
"Where's the fish? Look, is that a fish?"	63
Martin said, "That isn't a fish. That's a big black fly."	74
Then Bob asked, "Look, what's that?"	80
He said, "That's a frog on a log."	88
Then Bob asked, "Look, what's that?"	94
At last Martin said, "Bob, that's a fish in the	104
stream."	105

SCORING	Write student's name and date, mark any errors, and record total passage errors and WCPM on this page.
ORAL READING FLUENCY	Start timing at the ★. Mark errors. Make a single slash in the text (/) at 60 seconds. Have the student complete the passage. If the student completes the passage in less than 60 seconds, have the student go back to the ★ and continue reading. Make a double slash in the text (//) at 60 seconds.
WCPM	Determine words correct per minute by subtracting errors from words read in 60 seconds.
PASS	The student scores no more than 2 errors on the first pass through the passage and reads 70 or more words correct per minute. Proceed to Unit E.
NO PASS	The student scores 3 or more errors on the first pass through the passage and/or reads 69 or fewer words correct per minute. Provide targeted practice, use the Unit D Extra Practice lessons, reteach, and/or provide a Jell-Well Review. Then retest.

ORAL READING FLUENCY PASSAGE

Tucker and Pip

★Tuck has fun in his yard. Tuck's sister, Pip, has   10

fun too. Tuck and Pip play in the sand. Grandfather got   21

the sand for Tuck when Mom and Dad adopted him. It was   33

a birthday gift one year ago.   39

When Tuck and Pip play in the yard, Mom works in   50

the garden. There are little trees and plants all across the 61

yard. Mom picks weeds all day. She gets in the muck and   73

mud. Yuck!   75

Today, Pip's dog dashes across the backyard. King   83

is the best dog. He is big and black. He plays in the yard 97

with Tuck, and Tuck hoots and grins. It is a fun day in the 111

backyard.   112

SCORING	Write student's name and date, mark any errors, and record total passage errors and WCPM on this page.
ORAL READING FLUENCY	Start timing at the ★. Mark errors. Make a single slash in the text (/) at 60 seconds. Have the student complete the passage. If the student completes the passage in less than 60 seconds, have the student go back to the ★ and continue reading. Make a double slash (//) in the text at 60 seconds.
WCPM	Determine words correct per minute by subtracting errors from words read in 60 seconds.
PASS	The student scores no more than 2 errors on the first pass through the passage and reads 75 or more words correct per minute. Proceed to Unit F.
NO PASS	The student scores 3 or more errors on the first pass through the passage and/or reads 74 or fewer words correct per minute. Provide targeted practice, use the Unit E Extra Practice lessons, reteach and/or provide a Jell-Well Review. Then retest.

ORAL READING FLUENCY PASSAGE

Camping in the Park

★My friends, my mother, and I went camping in the   10

park. The park was a mix of green plants and forest. We   22

visited the park in the spring.   28

Mother had filled a box with food. We had lots and   39

lots to eat. Then we ran and jumped on the great big hill.   52

Matt said, "What if this hill was a volcano?" It was just a   65

hill, but it was fun to play.   72

Bill said, "Can you feel the Earth quiver and jiggle?   82

Quick! Run!" We ran about until it was dark.   91

Mother got a big quilt from the car, and we   101

looked at the stars. What fun! I will remember this   111

fantastic trip forever.   114

SCORING **ORAL READING** **FLUENCY**	Write student's name and date, mark any errors, and record total passage errors and WCPM on this page. Start timing at the ★. Mark errors. Make a single slash in the text (/) at 60 seconds. Have the student complete the passage. If the student completes the passage in less than 60 seconds, have the student go back to the ★ and continue reading. Make a double slash in the text (//) in the text at 60 seconds.
WCPM	Determine words correct per minute by subtracting errors from words read in 60 seconds.
PASS	The student scores no more than 2 errors on the first pass through the passage and reads 80 or more words correct per minute. Proceed to Unit G.
NO PASS	The student scores 3 or more errors on the first pass through the passage and/or reads 79 or fewer words correct per minute. Provide targeted practice, use the Unit F Extra Practice lessons, reteach and/or provide a Jell-Well Review. Then retest.

ORAL READING FLUENCY PASSAGE

The Lost Ring

★I had a ring. I lost it at the zoo. I asked   12

people, "Have you seen my ring?"   18

Alexander said, "I'm a detective! I will solve the   27

Case of the Missing Ring!"   32

Alexander and I went looking for my ring. We   41

made a list of where I had been. We looked near the   53

plants. We looked in the weeds. My brother Zack   62

came up to me. He asked, "What are you doing?"   72

I said, "Alexander is helping me look for my ring.   82

He is a great detective."   87

Zack said, "That is funny. Did you forget? Your   96

ring is in your zipper pocket!"   102

Alexander said, "The case is solved!"   108

I was happy to have my ring back.   116

SCORING **ORAL READING** **FLUENCY**	Write student's name and date, mark any errors, and record total passage errors and WCPM on this page. Start timing at the ★. Mark errors. Make a single slash in the text (/) at 60 seconds. Have the student complete the passage. If the student completes the passage in less than 60 seconds, have the student go back to the ★ and continue reading. Make a double slash in the text (//) in the text at 60 seconds.
WCPM	Determine words correct per minute by subtracting errors from words read in 60 seconds.
PASS	The student scores no more than 2 errors on the first pass through the passage and reads 82 or more words correct per minute. Proceed to Unit H.
NO PASS	The student scores 3 or more errors on the first pass through the passage and/or reads 81 or fewer words correct per minute. Provide targeted practice, use the Unit G Extra Practice lessons, reteach, and/or provide a Jell-Well Review. Then retest.

ORAL READING FLUENCY PASSAGE

Wiggy Weasel Plays Ball

★ My name is Wiggy Weasel. I am a reporter.	9
When I'm not working, I like to play ball. I think	20
my team is the best one in town.	28
My team works hard. We play on sunny days	37
and on cloudy days. We laugh and have a fantastic	47
time. Sometimes it rains, but we play even if the	57
ground is wet. If there is a hailstorm or a strong wind,	69
then we quit.	72
What do I like about baseball? I like playing with	82
my friends. I like the sound of the bat hitting the ball.	94
Whack! Crack! I like running the bases too.	102
Sometimes we travel to a nearby town to play.	111
We don't win every time, but we have lots of fun.	122

SCORING	Write student's name and date, mark any errors, and record total passage errors and WCPM on this page.
ORAL READING FLUENCY	Start timing at the ★. Mark errors. Make a single slash in the text (/) at 60 seconds. Have the student complete the passage. If the student completes the passage in less than 60 seconds, have the student go back to the ★ and continue reading. Make a double slash (//) in the text at 60 seconds.
WCPM	Determine words correct per minute by subtracting errors from words read in 60 seconds.
PASS	The student scores no more than 2 errors on the first pass through the passage and reads 85 or more words correct per minute. Proceed to Unit I.
NO PASS	The student scores 3 or more errors on the first pass through the passage and/or reads 84 or fewer words correct per minute. Provide targeted practice, use the Unit H Extra Practice lessons, reteach and/or provide a Jell-Well Review. Then retest.

ORAL READING FLUENCY PASSAGE

The Best Gardeners

★Chaz is a fantastic gardener. He helps other	8
people with their plants.	12
One day, I wished for a lot of beans to munch.	23
Chaz helped me plant some seeds in a pail. When it	34
didn't rain, I watered the seeds. When the seeds didn't	44
grow, Chaz gave the seeds notes. The notes said,	53
"Little seeds, you must get bigger."	59
I said, "Chaz, that is foolish. Seeds cannot read."	68
Then one sunny day, the seeds began to sprout.	77
I gave them more water, and then I weeded the ground	88
nearby. Chaz sent the little seedlings even more	96
notes.	97
In the spring, there were small beans on the	106
plants. Soon the beans were as tall as Chaz. We	116
were all speechless. Everyone said, "You and Chaz	124
are outstanding gardeners!"	127

SCORING	Write student's name and date, mark any errors, and record total passage errors and WCPM on this page.
ORAL READING FLUENCY	Start timing at the ★. Mark errors. Make a single slash in the text (/) at 60 seconds. Have the student complete the passage. If the student completes the passage in less than 60 seconds, have the student go back to the ★ and continue reading. Make a double slash (//) in the text at 60 seconds.
WCPM	Determine words correct per minute by subtracting errors from words read in 60 seconds.
PASS	The student scores no more than 2 errors on the first pass through the passage and reads 88 or more words correct per minute. Proceed to Unit J.
NO PASS	The student scores 3 or more errors on the first pass through the passage and/or reads 87 or fewer words correct per minute. Provide targeted practice, use the Unit I Extra Practice lessons, reteach, and/or provide a Jell-Well Review. Then retest.

ORAL READING FLUENCY PASSAGE

Chester Likes to Fly

★Chester is a little bird. When Chester was first　　9

born, he did not want to fly. Now Chester likes to fly high　　22

in the sky. He likes to fly with his brothers and sisters.　　34

Chester took a flight over the sea. He could see　　44

sand sharks and bright red fish.　　50

Chester took a flight over a farm. He could see　　60

chickens, cows, and sheep.　　64

Chester said, "Now I understand why mother　　71

wanted me to fly."　　75

Chester said to his brothers and sisters, "Let's fly　　84

over the park." Chester liked to see the kids play　　94

baseball. "Wow, look at that girl bat the ball," said　　104

Chester. "She seems very happy."　　109

Chester said, "I like being a bird. I like to fly over　　121

the land and the sea. I am happy too."　　130

SCORING	Write student's name and date, mark any errors, and record total passage errors and WCPM on this page.
ORAL READING FLUENCY	Start timing at the ★. Mark errors. Make a single slash in the text (/) at 60 seconds. Have the student complete the passage. If the student completes the passage in less than 60 seconds, have the student go back to the ★ and continue reading. Make a double slash in the text (//) at 60 seconds.
WCPM	Determine words correct per minute by subtracting errors from words read in 60 seconds.
PASS	The student scores no more than 2 errors on the first pass through the passage and reads 90 or more words correct per minute. Second grade students: Proceed to *Read Well 2*, Unit 1. Third and fourth grade students: Proceed to *Read Well 1 Plus*.
NO PASS	The student scores 3 or more errors on the first pass through the passage and/or reads 89 or fewer words correct per minute. Provide targeted practice, use the Unit J Extra Practice lessons, reteach and/or provide a Jell-Well Review. Then retest.

　　　　

Adams, M. J. (1990). *Beginning to read: Thinking and learning about print.* Cambridge, MA: MIT Press.

Anderson, L. W., Krathwohl, D. R., Airasian, P. W., Cruikshank, K. A., Mayer, R. E., Pintrich, P. R., Raths, J., & Wittrock, M. C. (2001). *Taxonomy for learning, teaching, and assessing: A revision of Bloom's Taxonomy of Educational Objectives.* New York: Longman.

Anderson, R. C., Hiebert, E., Scott, J., & Wilkinson, I. (1985). Becoming a nation of readers: The report of the commission on reading. Washington, DC: The National Institute of Education.

Archer, A. (2001, January 9). *New Mexico's mission to read.* Speech presented for the Statewide Professional Development for Reading, Albuquerque, NM.

Armbruster, B. B., Lehr, F., & Osborn, J. (2001). *Put reading first: The research building blocks for teaching children to read.* Washington, DC: National Institute for Literacy.

———. (2003) *Put reading first: The research building blocks for teaching children to read* (2nd ed.). Washington, DC: National Institute for Literacy.

Baker, S. K., Simmons, D. C., & Kame'enui, E. J. (1998). Vocabulary acquisition: Research bases. In D. Carnine & E. Kame'enui (eds.), *What reading research tells us about children with diverse learning needs: Bases and basics* (pp. 183–217). Mahwah, NJ: Lawrence Erlbaum Associates.

Baker, S. K., Kame'enui, E. J., Simmons, D. C., & Stahl, S. A. (1994). Beginning reading: Educational tools for diverse learners. *School Psychology Review, 23,* 372–391.

Baumann, J. F., & Bergeron, B. (1993). Story map instruction using children's literature: Effects on first graders' comprehension of narrative elements. *Journal of Reading Behavior, 25*(4), 407–437.

Baumann, J. F., & Kame'enui, E. J. (1991). Research on vocabulary instruction: Ode to Voltaire. In J. Flood, J. Jensen, D. Lapp, & J. R. Squire (eds.), Handbook of research on teaching the English language arts (pp. 604–632). New York: Macmillan.

Baumann, J. F., Kame'enui, E. J., & Ash, G. E. (2003). Research on vocabulary instruction: Voltaire redux. In J. Flood, D. Lapp, J. R. Squire, & J. M. Jenson (eds.), Handbook of research on teaching the English language arts (2nd ed.) pp. 752–785. Mahwah, NJ: Lawrence Erlbaum.

Beck, I. L., & McKeown, M. G. (1981). Developing questions that promote comprehension: The story map. *Language Arts, 58*(8), 913–918.

———. (2001). Text talk: Capturing the benefits of read-aloud experiences for young children. *The Reading Teacher, 55*(1), 10–20.

———. (2006). *Improving comprehension with questioning the author: A fresh and expanded view of a powerful approach.* New York: Scholastic Inc.

Beck, I. L., McKeown, M. G., & Kucan, L. (2002). *Bringing words to life: Robust vocabulary instruction.* New York: Guilford Press.

———. (2003, Spring). Taking delight in words: Using oral language to build young children's vocabularies. *American Educator, 27*(1), 36–46.

Beck, I. L., McKeown, M. G., Hamilton, R. L., & Kucan, L. (1997). *Questioning the author: An approach for enhancing student engagement with text.* Newark, DE: International Reading Association.

Beck, I. L., Omanson, R. C., & McKeown, M. G. (1982). An instructional redesign of reading lessons: Effects on comprehension. *Reading Research Quarterly 17*(4), 462–481.

Biemiller, A. (1999). *Language and reading success: From reading research to practice* (Vol. 5). Cambridge, MA: Brookline Books.

———. (2000). Vocabulary: The missing link between phonics and comprehension. *Perspectives, 26*(4), 26–30.

———. (2001, Spring). Teaching vocabulary: Early, direct, and sequential. *American Educator, 25,* 24–28.

———. (2003, Spring). Oral comprehension sets the ceiling on reading comprehension. *American Educator, 27*(1), 23, 44.

Carnine, D., Silbert, J., & Kame'enui, E. (1990). *Direct instruction reading*. Columbus, OH: Merrill Publishing.

Chall, J. S., & Jacobs, V. A. (Spring, 2003). Poor children's fourth-grade slump. *American Educator, 27*(1), 14–29.

Chall, J. S., Jacobs, V. A., & Baldwin, L. E. (1990). *The reading crisis: Why poor children fall behind*. Cambridge, MA: Harvard University Press.

Cudd, E. T., & Roberts, L. (1989). Using writing to enhance content area learning in the primary grades. *The Reading Teacher, 42*(6), 392–404.

Cunningham, P. M. (1998). The multisyllabic word dilemma: Helping students build meaning, spell, and read "big" words. *Reading and Writing Quarterly: Overcoming Learning Difficulties, 14*(2), 189–218.

Denton, C. A., Anthony, J. L., Parker, R., & Hasbrouck, J. E. (2004). Effects of two tutoring programs on the English reading development of Spanish-English bilingual students. *The Elementary School Journal, 104*(4), 289–305.

Dowhower, S. L. (1987). Effects of repeated reading on second grade transitional readers' fluency and comprehension. *Reading Research Quarterly, 22*, 389–406

———. (1991). Speaking of prosody: Fluency's unattended bedfellow. *Theory Into Practice, 30*, 165–175.

Duke, N. K. (2004). The Case for Informational Text. *Educational Leadership, 61*(6), 40–44.

Ehri, L. C., Nunes, S. R., Willows, D. M., Schuster, B. V., Yaghoub-Zadeh, Z., & Shanahan, T. (2001). Phonemic awareness instruction helps students learn to read: Evidence from the National Reading Panel's meta-analysis. *Reading Research Quarterly, 36*(3), 250–287.

Foorman, B. R., & Torgesen, J. (2001). Critical elements of classroom and small-group instruction promote reading success in all children. *Learning Disabilities: Research & Practice, 16*(4), 203–212.

Foorman, B. R., Francis, D. J., Fletcher, J. M., Mehta, P., & Schatschneider, C. (1998). The role of instruction in learning to read: Preventing reading failure in at-risk children. *Journal of Educational Psychology, 90*(1), 37–55.

Francis, D. J., Rivera, M., Lesaux, N., Kieffer, M., & Rivera, H. (2006). *Practical guidelines for the education of English language learners: Research-based recommendations for instruction and academic interventions*. Houston, TX: Center on Instruction.

Fry, E. B., Kress, J. E., & Fountoudis, D. L. (2000). *The reading teacher's book of lists*. San Francisco, CA: Jossey-Bass.

Fuchs, L. S., Fuchs, D., Hosp, M. K., & Jenkins, J. R. (2001). Oral reading fluency as an indicator of reading competence: A theoretical, empirical, and historical analysis. *Scientific Studies of Reading, 5*(3), 239–256.

Fuchs, D., Fuchs, L. S., Thompson, A., Al Otaiba, S., Yen, L., Yang, N. J., Braun, M., & O'Connor, R. (2001). Is reading important in reading-readiness programs? A randomized field trial with teachers as program implementers. *Journal of Educational Psychology, 93*(2), 251–267.

Gersten, R., Baker, S. K., Shanahan, T., Linan-Thompson, S., Collins, P., & Scarcella, R. (2007). *Effective literacy and English language instruction for English learners in the elementary grades*. Washington, DC: National Center for Education Evaluation and Regional Assistance Institute for Education Sciences, U.S. Department of Education.

Good, R. H., Wallin, J., Simmons, D. C., Kame'enui, E. J., & Kaminski, R. A. (2002). System-wide percentile ranks for DIBELS benchmark assessment (Technical Report #9). Eugene, OR: University of Oregon.

Hart, B., & Risley, T. (1995). *Meaningful differences in the everyday experience of young American children*. Baltimore, MD: Brookes Publishing.

Hasbrouck, J., & Tindal, G. (2005). Oral reading fluency: 90 years of measurement (Technical Report #33). Eugene, OR: University of Oregon, College of Education, Behavioral Research and Teaching.

Hirsch, E. D. (2003, Spring). Reading comprehension requires knowledge—of words and the world. *American Educator, 27*, 10–48.

Honig, B., Diamond, L., & Gutlohn, L. (2000). *CORE teaching reading sourcebook for kindergarten through eighth grade.* Novato, CA: Arena Press.

International Reading Association and National Association for the Education of Young Children (1998). Learning to read and write. Developmentally appropriate practices for young children. *The Reading Teacher, 52,* 193–216.

LaBerge, D., & Samuels, S. J. (1974). Toward a theory of automatic processing. *Cognitive Psychology, 6,* 293–323.

Logan, D. (1997). Automaticity and reading: Perspectives from the instance theory of automatization. *Reading and Writing Quarterly, 13,* 123–146.

McKeown, M. G., & Beck, I. L. (2004). Direct and Rich Vocabulary Instruction. In J. F. Baumann & E. J. Kame'enui (eds.). *Vocabulary Instruction,* p. 21. New York: The Guilford Press.

National Association for the Education of Young Children. (1985). *Learning to read and write: Developmentally appropriate practices for young children.* Washington, DC: National Association for the Education of Young Children.

National Reading Panel. (2000). Report of the national reading panel. Washington, DC: National Institute of Child Health and Human Development.

Ogle, D. (1986). K-W-L: A teaching model that develops active reading of expository text. *The Reading Teacher, 39,* 564–570.

Osborn, J., Lehr, F., & Hiebert, E. H. (2003). *A focus on fluency.* Honolulu, HI: Pacific Resources for Education and Learning.

Rayner, K., Foorman, B. R., Perfetti, C. A., Pesetsky, D., & Seidenberg, M. S. (2001). How psychological science informs the teaching of reading. *Scientific American, 2*(2), 31–74.

Rosenshine, B. (1997). Advances in Research on Instruction. In J. W. Lloyd, E. J. Kame'enui, & D. Chard (eds.), *Issues in educating students with disabilities,* pp. 197–221. Mahwah, NJ: Lawrence Erlbaum.

Samuels, S. J., & Flor, R. F. (1997). The importance of automaticity for developing expertise in reading. *Reading and Writing Quarterly, 13,* 107–121.

Santoro, L. E., Chard, D. J., Howard, L., & Baker, S. K. (2008). Making the very most of classroom read-alouds to promote comprehension and vocabulary. *The Reading Teacher, 61*(5), 396–408.

Snow, C. E., Burns, M. S., & Griffin, P. (eds.) (1998). Preventing reading difficulties in young children. Washington, DC: National Academy Press.

Sprick, R., Garrison, M., & Howard, L. (1998). *Champs: A proactive and positive approach to classroom management.* Longmont, CO: Sopris West.

Stahl, S. A. (2003). How words are learned incrementally over multiple exposures. *American Educator, 27*(1), 18–19, 44.

Torgesen, J. K. (2004). Avoiding the devastating downward spiral: The evidence that early intervention prevents reading failure. *American Educator, 28*(3), 6–19.

Vaughn, S., & Linan-Thompson, S. (2004). *Research-based methods of reading instruction, grades K–3.* Alexandria, VA: Association for Supervision and Curriculum Development.

What Works Clearinghouse; Institute of Education Sciences, U.S. Department of Education. (2006). Read Well. What Works Clearinghouse Intervention Report. Washington, DC: U.S. Department of Education (ED493775).

Woodcock, R. W. (1998). *Woodcock Reading Mastery Tests—Revised.* Circle Pines, MN: American Guidance Service.